JN436440

Birds, Flowers and Men

Selected Poems of

Kee-Chul Lee

Birds, Flowers and Men:
Selected Poems of Kee-Chul Lee

Published by
The Yeungnam University Press
2019

214-1, Gyeongsan City, Gyeongsangbuk-do
(Tel) 053-810-1801-4 (Fax) 053-810-4722
http://book.yu.ac.kr

First Published
10 January 2019

US$19.95
₩22.000

Book Design: Jae-Wan Jeong jjwankk@gmail.com

ISBN 978-89-7581-581-2 03810

이 도서의 국립중앙도서관 출판예정도서목록(CIP)은 서지정보유통지원시스템 홈페이지(http://seoji.nl.go.kr)와 국가자료종합목록시스템(http://www.nl.go.kr/kolisnet)에서 이용하실 수 있습니다. (CIP제어번호 : CIP2018037459)

Birds, Flowers and Men

Selected Poems of

Kee-Chul Lee

Parallel Texts in
Korean and English
Translated by
Jeo-Yong Noh

Yeungnam University Press

붉은 옷 한 벌 해지면 떠나갈 꽃들처럼
그렇게는 내게 온 생을 떠나보낼 수 없다

머리말

이 시집에 실린 대부분의 시는 지금까지 내가 낸 18권의 시집 가운데서 직접 뽑은 것이다. 이 시들은 오랫동안 내가 시작을 하면서 강한 애착을 느껴 온 서정시편들이다. 나는 지금까지 거의 반세기에 걸쳐 시를 쓰고 있다. 오래라면 오래인 나의 시의 길은 내가 생애를 다하는 날까지 지속되겠지만, 나는 내 시의 도정이 <서정을 꽃 피우는 길>이라는 생각에서 벗어난 일이 없다. 그러나 나는 나의 <서정시>가 옛날 옷을 벗고 새 옷을 갈아입어야 한다고 생각하면서 시를 써왔다. <서정시의 새 옷>, 그것은 까닭 없는 비탄, 값싼 감상(感傷)의 노출, 대상이 없는 하소연, 질 낮은 사랑의 어휘들의 남용을 금기로 하고 삶의 진실이 담긴 품격 있는 시의 위의(威儀)를 살리는 길이라 믿는다.

돌이켜 보면 나는 초기에는 <자연>을 많이 노래했고 중기에는 <생명>을 더 많이 노래했다. 그러나 지금은 <사람> 그리고 <인간관계>가 더 큰 주제가 되고 있는 듯하다. 나의 시에 점염되어 있는 사색과 고뇌, 연민과 애린, 그리고 자성과 희망의 언어들은 생래적인 것이면서도 내가 늘 곁에 두고 만지고 다듬은 보석들이다. 그러기에 지금도 나는 <상처의 보석>이 된 이 언어들을 사랑한다.

Like flowers—when a suit of red clothes wears out—
to be gone,
I cannot let my life depart from me.

Foreword

Most of the poems in this collection are chosen by my own hands from eighteen volumes that I have published until now. The selected poems are largely lyrics that I have felt a strong affinity throughout my long poetic career. As long as my writing goes along up to the end of my life, I will never stop thinking that the journey of my career is to make poetic lyricism blossoming. Believing that lyrics should take off old clothes and put on new ones, I have composed my poems. "The new clothes of lyrics"–that is nothing but to revive a poetic dignity by imbedding a shard of truth from life into a poem, I believe, while avoiding a groundless agony, the exposure of trite sentimentalism, whining and the dismal words of love.

In retrospect, my poems were much concerned with "nature" in the early phase. In the middle phase, they were rather saturated with "life". However, in the last phase my poems have been increasingly concerned with "men" and "human relations". Thought and agony, pity and love of a neighbour, and the words

내 시를 영역하는 노고를 아끼지 않은 영문학자 노저용 교수께 고마움 전하며, 남쪽으로 창을 낸 그의 화림동(花林洞) 서재에 햇빛이 많이 내리기를 바란다.

2018년 12월
이기철(李起哲)

of introspection and hope imbued in my poems are from my inborn traits; those are gems that I have felt with my fingers and refined all the time. Therefore, I still love those words which have turned themselves into “the gems of wound”.

I wish to express my gratitude to Professor Jeo-Yong Noh for his tireless efforts for accurate rendering my poems into English. Also I wish his fine library in the Hwarimdong valley with the windows to the south has more sunlight.

December 2018

Kee-Chul Lee

Acknowledgements

The translator wishes to record his deep gratitude to the poet Kee-Chul Lee who has helped the translator to understand his poems for several years through many profitable conversations and an exchange of numerous letters to ensure that the poems are both accurate and poetic in English translation. Indeed, this volume has been produced with the assumption that it is the translator's aim in translating poetry to be faithfully accurate to the original text and at the same time to make translations that read well as poems in their own right. This dual aim is not always easy to maintain and sometimes contradictory. In that case, the translator has tried to evade the word-for-ward translation with a belief that a translated work is not a shadow of an original text but a new created work.

The translator also wishes to express his many thanks to Professor Seong Woo Lim, Director of the Yeungnam University Media and Press Center, who has encouraged him by giving an opportunity to carry out this reluctant work of literary translation. Acknowledgements are due to Professor Jae-Wan Jeong from the Dept of Visual Communication Design, College of Design and Art from Yeungnam University, for his design of this volume and Mr. Jongbaek Lee, Editor-in-Chief of the Yeungnam University Media and Press Center, who has been patient until the corrections in the manuscripts have been satisfactorily made.

Table of Contents

머리말	Foreword	04

『청산행』(1982)에서 from *Lines Composed for the Blue Mountains*

청산행	Lines Composed for the Blue Mountains	16
월동엽서	A Postcard for Wintering	18
이향(離鄕)	Leaving Hometown	20
초록을 보며	Looking at Green	24
옛날의 금잔디	Old Golden Grass	26
고향	Hometown	28
이른 봄	Early Spring	30
작은 꽃	Little Flower	32

『우수의 이불을 덮고』(1988)에서 from *Covering with the Quilt of Melancholy*

우수의 이불을 덮고	Covering with the Quilt of Melancholy	36

『내 사랑은 해지는 영토에』(1989)에서 from *My Love Is in the Realm Where the Sun Sets*

좋은 날이 오면	If a Fine Day Comes	40

『지상에서 부르고 싶은 노래』(1993)에서 from *Song That I Wish to Sing on Earth*

정신의 열대	The Tropics of Spirit	44
멱라의 길 1	The Way to the Milou 1	48
불행도 더러 이웃이 되어	Even Infelicity Often Becomes a Neighbour	52
지상의 길	A Pathway on Earth	56
아름다운 사람	A Living Soul of Beauty	60
물 긷는 사람	One Who Is Drawing Water	64
지상에서 부르고 싶은 노래 1	Song That I Wish to Sing on Earth 1	68
봄밤	Night in Springtime	72
햇볕이 되었거나 노을이 되었거나	Whether It Was Either Sunlight or Sunglow	76
산길 물길	A Mountain Pass, a Waterway	78
땅 위의 이름을 사랑하네	I Love Names on Earth	80
마흔 살의 동화	A Fairy Tale at Forty	84
세상 속으로	Into the World	88

『열하를 향하여』(1995)에서 from *Towards Jehol*

생의 노래	Song of Life	92
열하를 향하여	Towards Jehol	96
서풍에 기대어 1	Standing against the West Wind	100
마음 속 푸른 이름	The Blue Name in Mind	104
작은 이름 하나라도	Even If a Little Name	106

『유리의 나날』(1998)에서 from *Days of Glass*

유리, 노래	Glass, A Song	112
유리에 닿는 길 1	A Pathway to Glass 1	114
유리의 나날 1	Days of Glass 1	118
유리의 나날 9—부석사에서	Days of Glass 9—At Buseoksa	122
유리에 묻는다	An Inquiry Is Made to Glass	126
내 안의 유리	Glass inside Me	128
유리, 마을—석리라는 곳	Glass, A Village—The Place Called Seok-ri	132
유리의 길 3	A Pathway to Glass 3	134

『내가 만난 사람은 모두 아름다웠다』(2000)에서 from *Those Whom I Have Met Were All Beautiful*

내가 만난 사람은 모두 아름다웠다	Those Whom I have Met Were All Beautiful	138
풀잎	Leaves of Grass	140
언제 삶이 위기 아닌 적 있었던가	Hasn't There Ever Been Life without a Crisis?	142
시	Poetry	144
돌에 대해서	Of a Stone	146
별까지는 가야 한다	Up to the Stars Must We Go	148
벚꽃 그늘에 앉아 보렴	Sit down in the Shade of Cherry Blossoms, Please	152
봄길과 동행하다	Accompanied by a Path in Springtime	156

『가장 따뜻한 책』(2005)에서 from *The Warmest Book*

별이 뜰 때	When Stars Twinkle	162
따뜻한 책	The Warm Book	166

『나무, 나의 모국어』(2012)에서 from *The Tree, My Mother Tongue*

가을이라는 물질	A Material Called Autumn	170
가을 우체국	A Post Office in Autumn	172

『꽃들의 화장 시간』(2014)에서 from *At the Makeup Hour of Flowers*

생은 과일처럼 익는다	Life Ripens Like the Fruit	176
그늘은 나무의 생각이다	A Bower Is the Idea of a Tree	178

『흰 꽃 만지는 시간』(2017)에서 from *A Time for Fondling the White Flower*

시간	Time	182
시인이 걷는 길이 가장 아름다운 길이 되었으면 좋겠다	I Wish the Poet's Path to Be a Fairest One	184
모르는 사람의 손이 더 따뜻하리라	Hands of a Stranger Will Be Warmer	186
스무 번째의 별 이름	Name of the Twentieth Star	188

흰 종이 위에	On the White Paper	190
목백일홍 옛집	An Old House with Crape-myrtle	192
나무를 눕히는 방법	A Way of Laying a Tree Down	194
채송화 수첩	A Jotter for Rose Moss	196

미수록 시편 from Uncollected Poems

근심을 지펴 밥을 짓는다	Cooking Rice by Burning Anxiety as Firewood	200
아침 언어	Words at Morn	204
새똥	Bird's Droppings	206

연보 Life and Works of Kee-Chul Lee 209

About the Translator 216

『청산행』(1982)에서

From *Lines Composed for the Blue Mountains*

청산행

손 흔들고 떠나갈 미련은 없다
며칠 째 청산에 와 발을 푸니
흐리던 산길이 잘 보인다
상수리 열매를 주우며 인가를 내려다보고
쓰다 둔 편지 구절과 버린 칫솔을 생각한다
남방으로 가다 길을 놓치고
두어 번 허우적거리는 여울물
산 아래는 때까치들이 몰려와
모든 야성을 버리고 들 가운데 순결해진다
길을 가다가 자주 뒤를 돌아보게 하는
서른 번 다져두고 서른 번 포기했던 관습들
서쪽 마을을 바라보면 나무들의 잔 숨결처럼
가늘게 흩어지는 저녁연기가
한 가정의 고민의 양식으로 피어오르고
생목 울타리엔 들거미줄
맨살 비비는 돌들과 함께 누워
실로 이 세상을 잃아보지 않은 것들과 함께
잠들고 싶다

Lines Composed for the Blue Mountains

I have no regrets for leaving, while waving a hand.
After a few days in the blue mountains to rest up,
the loomed mountain path looks clear in view.
Picking up acorns, I look down at the houses
and bethink a phrase in an unfinished letter
    and a dumped toothbrush.
Going astray in running southward,
the rapids turn and twist two or three times.
Butcherbirds swarming at the foot of the mountain
lose all of their wild nature and get chaste in the field.
The customs that often made me look back on my way
and that braced myself thirty times and giving up thirty times:
when I look westward at a village,
an evening smoke drifting like a placid breath of trees
rises up as a pattern of domestic anxiety.
Lying down under a hedge spun by a spider's web
and with stones rubbing their bare skin,
I wish to fall asleep with things
that have never been truly sick with this world.

월동엽서

순이, 손을 몇 번 불어서 그 겨울은 지나갔나
미나리 잎새 얼어서 얼음 밑에 묻혀 있던 그 겨울
장작개비 책보에 얹고 가던 등교 길
소백산맥 끝 웅크린 골짜기
너는 전근가는 아버질 따라 진준가 사천인가로
닳은 고무신을 끄을며 떠났지만
얼음이 얼다 녹던 축축한 뫼부리에 앉아
마른 잔디만 집어 뜯던 나는 지금
허언을 괴로워하는 삐걱이는 강의실 계단을 오르내린다
스물을 지나 서른이 되어서 너의 그 검정치마도
세상따라 모양이 달라졌겠지만
진준가 사천인가의 언덕 아래 조그만 마을에서
너는 이제 두 번째 아이를 낳고
들길에 나가 너의 아이들에게
새로 핀 꽃이름을 가르치고 있는가
이 겨울 난로 꺼지면 나는 양말을 갈아 신고
저 죽은 풀빛의 들판이나 밟으면서
겨울의 가장 따뜻한 곳으로 걸어가야겠다
눈이 내리면 다시 시린 손을 불며

A Postcard for Wintering

Suni, how many times did you blow on your hands to pass
    that winter
when the frozen leaves of water parsley were buried under ice?
On the way to school with a bundle of books loaded
    by the pieces of firewood,
and a hunched gorge at the tip of the Sobaek mountain range.
Though you, dragging on your old rubber shoes, went after
your father who was transferred to Jinju or Sacheon,
I, once sitting on the damp top of a mountain melted from ice
and plucking a dry grass only, now go up and down
the creaking stairs of a lecture room tortured by falsehood.
Coming into the thirties after the twenties,
you may have changed the fashion of your long black skirt
    while taking the world as it is, though;
in a small village at the foot of a hill in Jinju or Sacheon,
now you gave birth to a second son.
Do you take your children to a field path
and teach them the names of newly bloomed flowers?
If a stove goes out this winter, I'll change my socks.
Treading on the dead greenish field,
I must walk on to the warmest place in winter.
If snow falls, again I'll breathe on my numb hands.

이향(離鄕)

제대를 하고 대학을 졸업하면
나는 개나리꽃이 한닷새 마을의 봄을 앞당기는
산난초 뿌리 풀리는 조그만 시골에서
시나 쓰는 가난한 서생이 되어 살려고 생각했다
고급장교가 되어 있는 초등학교 동창과
개인회사 중역이 되어 있는 어릴 적 친구들이 모두 마을을 떠날 때
나는 다시 이 마을로 돌아와 탱자나무 울타리를 손질하는
초부가 되어 살려고 생각했다
눈 속에서 지난 해 지워진 쓴냉이 잎새가 새로 돋고
물레방앗간 뒤쪽에 비비새가 와서 물면
간호원을 하러 독일로 떠난 여자 친구의 항공엽서나 기다리며
느린 하학종을 울리는 낙엽송 교정에서
잠처럼 조용한 풍금소리를 듣는 이급정교사가 되어 살려고 생각했다
용서할 줄 모르는 시간은 물처럼 흘러갔고
놀 속에 묻히는 봄보리들의 침묵이 무섭게 나를 위협했을 때
관습의 신발 속에 맨발을 꽂으며 나는
눈에 익은 수많은 돌멩이들의 정분을 거역하기 시작했다
염소들 불러 모으는 비음의 말들과
부피가 작은 국정교과서를 거역하기 시작했다
뒷산에 홀로 누운 할아버지의 산소를 한 번만 바라보았고
그리고는 뛰는 버스에 올라 도시 속의 먼지가 되었다
봄이 오면 아직도 그 골의 물소리와 아이들의 자치기 소리가

Leaving Hometown

If I was discharged from the army and graduated from a college,
I planned to live, as a poor literatus dabbling in poetry, in a small
village where forsythia heralds springtime about five days earlier
and where the roots of a wild orchid get untangled.
When my primary school alumni, a high-ranking military officer
or a company director or other friends, left the village in their
childhood, I planned to return to this village again and to live
as a woodcutter trimming the trifoliate orange tree.
When a bitter cress crushed last year sprouts anew in snow
and parrotbills chirp behind a water mill, I was to live
as a second-grade regular teacher listening to a quiet organ
like slumber, while waiting for an airmail from my girl friend
who went to Germany to be a nurse or while listening to
a resounding dismissal bell on the larch campus.
An unforgivable time has run just like a stream.
When the silence of spring barley buried under an evening glow
terribly threatened me, I, thrusting my bare feet into the shoes
of customs, began to defy an intimacy of numerous familiar stones.
I began to defy the words of a nasal twang calling goats
and a slim volume of the government designated textbook.
Once glancing at my grandfather's lonely grave on the hill behind
the village,

도시의 옆구리에 잠든 나의 꿈 속에
배달되지 않은 엽신으로 녹아
문지방을 울리며 흐르고 있다

I became a speck of dust in the city by getting on a rushing bus.
When spring comes, the sound of water in a dell and the noise of
    children's playing tipcat,
melted as an undelivered leaf blade in my dream after fallen asleep
    in the flank of city,
are still running, whilst resounding the threshold.

초록을 보며

돌자갈 마꽃 수세미들의 하늘은 아직 쓸쓸하다
들판에는 몇 번을 지워졌다 피는 풀꽃
길들은 언제나 서성이면서 南으로 벋어 있고
모래들 흩어지고 산들은 허리 잘려
그리움 많은 사람들의 봄도 강물에 조금씩
숨긴 맘 풀어놓는다
여기저기 추억의 얼룩처럼 돋는 풀잎, 그러나
초록의 얼굴은 오래가지 않는다
지상에는 대부분 단명한 것들
상처의 보석을 사랑하는 사람들의 깊은 침묵 속으로
들새들 행방 감추며 길게 날고
산들은 이 봄에 엄청난 無知로도
도라지꽃을 피워놓고 혼자 잠든다
조그맣고 정결한 삶 하날 찾기 위해
우리는 또 몇 천리의 길을 걸어야 하나
金言과 망각의 고통스런 뒤섞임 뒤로
양심과 휴지조각과 두어겹 부끄러움 숨겨두고
흐려진 불빛 세워 잠든 마을 바라보면
천의 바람 끝에 실낱처럼 흩어지는
슬픔의 섬세한 얼굴이 보인다

Looking at Green

The sky of yam flowers and vegetable sponges is still forlorn.
In the field, there are the grass flowers falling and blooming again.
The lingering road always stretches out to the south
and the sand is scattered and the mountainsides are cut off.
For those who have yearnings, spring untangles
their hidden mind little by little into the river.
Here and there, the leaves of grass sprout like a stain of memory,
but a face of green does not last long.
Most of things on earth die young.
Into the deep silence of those who love the jewels of the wound
take the wild birds hiding their whereabouts a long flight.
This spring, the mountains fall into sleep by itself
after letting balloonflowers bloom in an awful ignorance.
Just to seek for a tiny, tidy life,
how many thousands-ri do we have to walk again?
Leaving a painful mix of adage and oblivion behind
and hiding conscience, a scrap of paper and a double-layered shame
—if I look at a village fallen asleep under the dim light—
I can see a subtle face of sadness at the tip
of a thousand winds scattering like a fine thread.

옛날의 금잔디

4월이 오면 살구꽃이 피는 마을로 가야지
죽은 강아지풀들이 다시 살아 일어나고
초가 추녀 끝에 물소리가 방울 울리는 마을로 가야지
풀밭에는 어릴 적 잃어버린 구슬이 고운 숨 할딱이며
누워 있겠지
이랑에는 철 만난 완두콩이 부지런히 제 몸에 푸른 물을 들이고
잠자던 뿌리들이 이제 막 흐르기 시작한 물 아래 내려가
물들의 가장 깊은 속살을 빨아먹겠지
눈썹에 앵두꽃을 단 처녀애들은
작년에 넣어둔 분홍신을 꺼내 신고 들판을 달리고
마을 사람들은 햇빛 보다 먼저 일어나
간격이 고른 녹색 대문을 집마다 달겠지
동구 길엔 비가 와도 젖지 않는 복숭아꽃이 피고
구르는 돌멩이도 부서져 제비풀의 거름이 되겠지
4월이 오면 혼자서도 외롭지 않은 옛날의 금잔디
거기 가서 휘파람 몇 가닥 남겨두고 와야지
거기 가서 댕기에 눈물 닦던 누님의 기침 소릴 듣고 와야지

Old Golden Grass

When April comes, I'll go to the village where an apricot blooms.
I'll go to the village where the dead leaves of foxtail rise again
and where water dripping on the edge of eaves of a thatched
    house is ringing.
In the field, a bead that I lost in my early years will be panting
in a tender breath while lying down.
Peas in season will be busy with dyeing them green in furrow
and the sleeping roots will descend under the newly flowing water
and suck the deepest quick of water.
Maidens who adorn cherry blossoms on eyebrows will wear
last year's pink shoes and dash across the field.
The village folk will get up before the sun rises up
and install a regular-spaced green gate at each house.
Although it rains, the peach tree, unwetted, will bloom
    at the entrance to the village
and a rolling stone will be broken and become muck for a violet.
If April comes, old golden grass is not lonely despite being alone.
I'll go there and come back after leaving a few tunes of whistle.
I'll go there and come back after hearing the coughing of my sister
    who would wipe her tears with a hair ribbon.

고향

신발을 벗지 않으면 건널 수 없는 내를 건너야
비로소 만나게 되는
불과 열 집 안팎의 촌락은 봄이면 화사했다
복숭아꽃이 바람에 떨어져도 아무도 알은 채를 안했다
아쉽다든지 안타깝다든지
양달에서는 작년처럼, 너무도 작년처럼
삭은 가랑잎을 뚫고 씀바귀 잎새가 새로 돋고
두엄 더미엔 자루가 부러진 쇠스랑 하나가
버려진 듯 꽂혀있다
발을 닦으며 바라보면
모래는 모래대로 송아지는 송아지대로
모두 제 생각에만 골똘했다
바람도 그랬다

Hometown

There is a hamlet consisting of about ten houses.
Crossing the beck, one is bound to face it at last:
    yet, if not taking off one's shoes, he cannot cross it.
Every springtime, the village is gorgeous.
When peach blossoms fell down by the winds,
    no one pretended to be aware of
whether it was sad or regretful.
In the sunny spot just as in the last year,
the new shoots of a sowthistle sprout from
    the rotten dead leaves
and the pitchfork with a broken handle is stuck up
amidst a heap of manure as if abandoned.
Washing up my feet, I looked out:
the sand was in the way of its own and a calf was
    in the same way of its own.
All were absorbed only in their own thinking.
The wind was the same, too.

이른 봄

마을로 들어오는 푸섶길에는 철 잃은 패랭이꽃 한 송이 피어 있다. 벌초도 하지 않은 무덤이 두엇 누워 있고 全州李公之墓, 이끼마저 말라붙은 묘비가 오래오래 그 모습대로 서 있다. 바람이 불 때 모로 슬리는 마른 풀잎들, 그 적막 가운데 잘못 피어난 한 잎 패랭이꽃. 연날리기 자치기 숨바꼭질 하는 아이들의 발길에도 밟히지 않고 누구도 뜻있게 이름 불러 주는 이 없는 이 작은 한 송이 들꽃, 자손도 儒林도 돌볼 사람 없는 폐허가 되어 버린 두엇의 무덤. 마을로 들어오는 산어귀엔 멎은 지 오래인 물레방아, 귀를 기울여도 들리지 않는 봄 나물 캐는 누이들의 부끄러운 愁心歌.

Early Spring

On the grassy track to the entrance of a village, a rainbow pink is unseasonably in bloom. A couple of graves covered with uncut grass lie in supine, and the grave of the venerable Yi from the Jeonju clan whose tombstone covered with dried moss stands as it used to be there long long ago. When the wind blows, the dried leaves chafe against the ground obliquely. In stillness, the rainbow pink is untimely in bloom. This little wild flower is untrodden by children who fly either kites or play the tipcat or play hide and seek. There is none who may call it by its name. The twosome ruined graves are deserted by the descendents and the Confucians. At the entrance to the village, the waterwheel at the gateway to the mountain ceased spinning long ago. Although my ears are strained to, the mournful song for the frailty of human life by the bashful sisters who gather wild greens in springtime
is unheard.

작은 꽃

차고 슬프게
바람에 불리우는 풀꽃들
이 세상 누구도 그의 이름을 부른 적 없어
마을 아이도 이름을 알지 못하는
하이얗고 순한 작은 꽃.
바람이 분다. 별이 뜬다.
조약돌이 물에 씻긴다.
밤이 가고 싸늘한 이마의
아침이 온다.
소리쳐도 들어 줄 이 없어
안타까움으로 혼자 서 있는
언젠가 가본 듯한 시골驛 부근의
이슬에 젖어 있는 작은 꽃.

Little Flower

In coldness and sadness,
blown are the flowering plants by the wind.
As no one in this world has called it by its name,
children in the village do not know of
the name of the meek, white flower.
The wind blows. Stars start twinkling.
Pebbles are washed by the water.
Night passes away
and morn comes with a chilly forehead.
It may cry out, but there is none who can hear it;
in pity, it stands alone near the country station
where once I have likely been to—
the dewy little flower.

『우수의 이불을 덮고』(1988)에서

From *Covering with the Quilt of Melancholy*

우수의 이불을 덮고

오늘도 우리 아는 이웃들은 다 무사합니다
자주 손끝에 덧나는 희망
오래 만져서 닳고 닳은 고통들은 잠들었습니다
누더기의 남쪽 산에 버짐 같은 꽃들은 지고
안부 없는 흰 새들 내를 건너 날아갔습니다
만나지 못한 사람의 이름만 아직도 열병처럼 이마를
두근거리고 있습니다
흙 속에 묻힌 옥잠화 씨앗은 제 혼자 따뜻하고
우리가 가장 쓸쓸할 때 부를 이름 하나는
아직 가슴 속에 남겨 두었습니다
그대 먼 길 가거든 돌아오지 마셔요
그대 못질한 문패와 뜨락의 신발들 다 잘 있습니다
뒷날 부를 노래 한 소절 베개 맡에 묻어두고
우수의 이불을 덮고 오늘 밤은 혼자 잠듭니다

Covering with the Quilt of Melancholy

Even today, all of our neighbours with whom we are acquainted
    are safe, too.
Often, hope gets inflected at its fingertips.
Pains worn-out by a tenacious touch are in sleep.
Like a ringworm, the flowers are gone on the ragged southern
    mountains
and white birds sending no greetings flew over the stream.
Only the names of men with whom I have never met
make my forehead still throbbing like a fever.
A seed of plantain lily buried in the soil is all warm to itself
and one name is left to call in our bosom.
when we are most lonesome.
If you go far away, don't come back.
The doorplate that you nailed and the shoes in garden are all well.
Storing a bar of song near a pillow to sing later,
I sleep alone under the quilt of melancholy, tonight.

『내 사랑은 해지는 영토에』(1989)에서

From *My Love Is in the Realm Where the Sun Sets*

좋은 날이 오면

좋은 날이 오면 아름다운 서정시 한 편 쓰리라
바라보기도 눈부신 좋은 날이 마침내 오기만 하면
네 맘 내 맘 모두 출렁이는 강물이 되는
기쁜 서정시 한 편 쓰고야 말리라
그때가 되면 끝없는 회의의 글을 읽고
번민의 숟가락 들지 않아도 되리라
돌 별 하늘 꽃나무만 노래해도 되리라
피 노호 상처 고통을 맑은 물에 헹궈
얼굴 맑은 누이 이름처럼 불러도 되리라
금빛 날을 짜서 만든 찬란한 한낮처럼
오래 가는 메아리처럼, 즐거운 추억처럼
루비 호박 에메랄드 사파이어처럼
잠을 밀어내는 젊은 날의 약속처럼
아, 좋은 날이 오면 잊었던 노래 한 구절
들 가운데서 불러보리라
이름 부르기조차 설레는 좋은 날이
대문과 지붕 위에 덮이기만 하면

If a Fine Day Comes

If a fine day comes, I'll compose a lyric of beauty.
If a brilliant day comes anyway after all,
I'll never fail to write a lyric of joy which makes
your mind and mine both turn into the rolling river.
If the day comes, there will be no need to read
endless sceptic writings or to lift a spoon of agony.
It'll be all right to sing of a stone, a star, the sky
    and a flowering tree only.
After blood, uproar, scars and pains are rinsed with
    clean water,
they can be called like the name of my clean-faced sister.
Like the radiant noon woven with golden light,
like a long lingering echo, like a merry memory,
like ruby, amber, emerald and sapphire
and like an appointment pushing out sleep in my youth,
ah, if a fine day comes,
I'll sing a bar of a forgotten song in the field.
If a fine day making my heart throbbing just by calling
the name covers over the gate and the roof only

『지상에서 부르고 싶은 노래』(1993)에서

From *Song That I Wish to Sing on Earth*

정신의 열대

내 정신의 열대, 멱라를 건너가면
거기 슬플 것 다 슬퍼해본 사람들이
고통을 씻어 햇볕에 널어 두고
쌀 씻어 밥 짓는 마을 있으리
더러 초록을 입에 넣으며 초록만큼 푸르러지는
사람들 살고 있으리
그들이 봄 강물처럼 싱싱하게 묻는 안부 내 들을 수 있으리

오늘 아침 배춧잎처럼 빛나던 청의를 물고
날아간 새들이여
네가 부리로 물고 가 짓는 삭정이집 아니라도
사람이 사는 집들
남으로만 흘러내리는 추녀들이
지붕 끝에 놀을 받아 따뜻하고
오래 아픈 사람들이 병을 이기고 일어나는
아이 울음처럼 신선한 뜨락 있으리

저녁의 고전적인 옷을 벗기고
처녀의 발등 같은 흰 물결 위에
살아서 깊어지는 노래 한 구절 보탤 수 있으리
오래 고통을 잠재우던 이불 소리와
아플 것 다 아파본 사람들의 마음 불러 모아

The Tropics of Spirit

If I cross over the Miluo river°, the tropics of my spirit,
there may be those who have gone through all sorts of sadness
and who have washed pain and have put it in the sun;
there may be a village where they wash rice and cook it.
There may be some people in living who become greenish
as much as greenness by putting greenness into their mouths.
I can hear their asking freshly after me like a stream in spring.

Birds, this morning holding in their beaks blue clothes shining
like Chinese cabbage leaves, are flown away!
It may not be a brushwood nest that you build with your beaks,
but it will be the houses in which men live.
The eaves running only southward are warm
by the glow of sunset reflected from the edge of the roof.
As if the sick beat a long illness and rose up,
there would be a refreshing yard like a baby's cry.

Undressing the classical robe of an evening,
I can add a line of song meaningful through living
onto the white waves looking like the top of the maiden's foot.
Summoning the sound of a quilt putting a long pain into sleep
and the minds of those who have had all sorts of pain,

고로쇠 숲에서 우는 청호반새의 노래를
인간이 가진 가장 아름다운 말로 번역할 수 있으리

내 정신의 열대 멱라°를 건너가면

° 멱라—중국 호남성에 있는 강 이름.

I can translate the songs of a black-capped kingfisher singing
in the grove of maple into the most beautiful words of a man.

If I crossed over the Milou river, the tropics of my spirit

° The Miluo river is famous for the location of the ritual suicide in 278 BC of Qu Yuan, a poet of Chu state during the Warring States period in China.

멱라의 길 1

걸어가면 지상의 어디에 멱라°가 흐르고 있을 것인데
나는 갈 수 없네. 산 첩첩 물 중중
사람이 수자리 보고 짐승의 눈빛 번개쳐
갈 수 없네
구강 장강 물 구비치나 언덕 무너뜨리지 않고
낙타를 탄 상인들은 욕망만큼 수심도 깊어
이 물가에 사금파리 같은 꿈을 묻었다
어디서 이소°° 한 가닥 바람에 불려오면
내 지상에서 얻은 병 모두 쓸어 저 강물에 띄우겠네

발목이 시도록 걸어가는 나날은
차라리 삶의 보석을 갈무리한다고
상강으로 드는 물들이 뒤를 돌아보며 주절대지만
문득 신발에 묻은 흙을 보며 멱라의 길이 꿈밖에
있음을 깨닫고
혼자 피었다 지는 꽃 한 송이에 눈 닿는 것도
이승의 인연이라 생각한다

일생이 아름다워서 아름다운 사람은 없다
일생이 노역과 상처 아문 자리로 얼룩져 있어도
상처를 길들이는 마음 고와서 아름다운 사람은 있다
때로 삶은 우리의 걸음을 비뚤어지게 하고

The Way to the Milou○ 1

If I walk along, somewhere the Milou may be flowing on earth;
yet I can't go. The mountains lie in layers and the water runs
ins and outs.
Men guard the frontier and the eyes of a beast strike like
the lightning, so I can't go.
The Jiujiang river○○ and the Yangtze wind their ways
but do not pull down the banks.
An anxiety of the merchants on camels is as deep as greed;
they buried their dreams like a piece of chinaware on this shore.
If a melody of Li Sao○○○ came along somewhere with the wind,
I would sweep up all sorts of disease from the world
and set them afloat on the river.

Although the water coming into the Xiang river○○○○ looks back
and rambles on my daily walking to be in store
for the gems of life until my ankles get asleep,
suddenly I, looking at the shoes smeared with soil
and realizing the way to the Milou lies outside my dream,
muse a flower within my eyeshot blooming and falling down
by itself is a nidana in this world.

No one is beautiful on account of the beauty of one's life.

독 묻은 역설을 아름답게 하지만
멱라 흐르는 물빛이 죽음마저도 되돌려주는지는 못한다
아무도 걸어온 제 발자국 헤아린 자 없어도
발자국 뒤에 남은 혈흔 쌓여
한 해가 되고 일생이 된다

° 멱라--중국 호남성에 있는 강 이름. 중국서정시의 효시인 초사(楚辭)를 시작한 전국시대 초나라의 굴원이 주위의 참소로 분함을 못 이겨 빠져 죽은 강으로 유명함. 여기서는 내 정신의 강으로 비유됨

° 시름을 만난다는 뜻으로 굴원이 멱라에 빠져 죽을 결심을 하기까지의 시름을 적은 장시(長詩).

Although life gets freaked with labour and scars,
there are lovely people whose hearts for tending scars are lovely.
Now and again, life twists our steps and makes a venomous
paradox lovely though,
the aquamarine of the flowing Milou does not retrieve even death.
There is none who has ever counted the number of footprints
in lifetime though, a bloodstain left behind files up
and turns it into a year and then a lifetime.

° The Milou river: Originating in Xiushui County of Jiangxi province, the river is famous for the location of the ritual suicide in 278 BC of Qu Yuan, a poet of Chu state during the Warring States period, in protest against the corruption of the era. In this poem, the Milou river is used as a metaphor for the poet's spirit.

°° The Jiujiang river: Jiujiang literally means "nine rivers". It is a prefecture-level city located on the southern shores of the Yangtze River in northwest Jiangxi Province, People's Republic of China.

°°° Li Sao (Chinese: 離騷; literally: "Encountering Worry") is a Chinese poem dating from the Warring States period of ancient China. This is a long poem which tells of the suicidal drowning of Qu Yuan who was a member of the Chu royal clan and served as an official under King Huai of Chu (reigned 328–299 BC).

°°°° The chief river of the Lake Dongting drainage system of the middle Yangtze, the largest river in Hunan Province in China. The river flows generally northeast through Guangxi and Hunan provinces.

불행도 더러 이웃이 되어

나는 불행을 감금시킬 빗장이 없다
불행은 오래 산 내 몸을 만나면
여름벌레처럼 날개 치며 잉잉거린다

배춧잎과 쌀의 혼숙인 나의 살
이불을 덮어주어도 추위 타는 정신의 임자몸인
내 육신 속으로
가끔은 발을 구르며 지나가는 불행이 보인다

윤기 나는 저녁의 나무들을 거쳐
검은 밤 속으로 흰 살을 빛내며 걸어가는
아직 처녀인 추억이여

이제 다 왔다, 그곳에 너의 닳은 신발을 묻어라
떠도는 빗방울에도 생애의 반쪽이 젖어
이 추위 다 가릴 수 있는 이불이 없다

노동과 치욕을 비벼 먹은 밥들이
살이 되는 나날을 뒤로하고
내가 걸어가야 하는 뭍은 어디인가

한 볏단도 땀 없이는 거둘 수 없음을

Even Infelicity Often Becomes a Neighbour

I have no latch bolting infelicity.
When infelicity meets with my long-lived body,
it buzzes like a summer insect flapping its wings.

My flesh is a room shared by Chinese cabbage leaves and rice.
Infelicity is often seen stamping its feet and passing
through my body, the master of spirit which is sensitive
to the cold, though it is covered with the quilt.

Through the lustrous trees in the evening into a dark night,
shining with the white flesh,
walks a still virgin memory!

Here you are now. Bury your worn-out shoes there.
As a half of lifetime is wet even by drifting raindrops,
there is no quilt to cover up this coldness completely.

Leaving behind the days that the boiled rice eaten up
by a mix of labour with disgrace turns into flesh,
where is the land that I have to walk on?

Autumn teaches me by sending a tinted leaf to me;

가을은 물든 잎을 보내 나에게 가르친다
누가 경전에서 깨우치겠는가
쟁반에 담기는 밥상 위의 김치가
삶을 가르치는 책장인 것을

a sheaf of rice cannot be reaped without sweat.
Who can become enlightened by the scriptures?
Kimchi on a plate at a dining table is the leaves of a book
teaching what life is.

지상의 길

얼마를 더 살면 여름을 떼어다가 가을에 붙여도
아프지 않은 흰구름 같은 무심을 배우랴
내 잠시 눈빛 주면 웃는 꽃들과
잠 깨어 이마 빛나는 돌들 곁에서
지금은 햇볕이 댕기보다 곱던 꽃들을 데리고 어둠 속으로 돌아가는 시간
절연의 아픔을 나는 여기서 본다

짐을 내려 놓아라, 이제 물의 몸이 잠시 쉬어야 한다
나를 따라오느라 발이여 너 고생했다
내일 나는 너에게 새 구두를 사주지 않으리
너는 육신의 명령을 거역한 일 없으므로

그러니 나는 가야한다, 한 번의 가을도 거짓으로 꽃피운 일 없는 들을 지나
작은 물줄기가 흐름을 시작하는 산을 지나
아직도 정신의 열대인 내 가혹한 시간 속으로
나는 가야한다

내 발 닿은 길 지상의 한 뼘밖에 안 돼
배추벌레 기어간 엽맥에 불과해도
내 불러야 할 즈믄 개의 이름들과 목숨들을 위해

A Pathway on Earth

How much longer am I to live to learn such indifference
    as the white clouds feeling no pain
When summer is ripped off and added to autumn?
Beside the smiling flowers that I give a wink at briefly
and the awakened stones whose foreheads are shining,
it's a time now that the sunlight takes back the flowers
which are prettier than a hair ribbon into the darkness;
    here, I feel a pang of separation.

Put down a load. Now the body of water should take
    a brief rest.
Feet, you have had trouble with tagging along with me!
Tomorrow, I won't buy you new shoes
because you have never disobeyed a bodily command.

But I have to go across the field that not a single autumn
    has once put forth blossoming falsely,
and to pass by the mountains where a little stream starts.
Into my cruel time, still the tropics of spirit,
I must go.

As the path that my foot can reach is but a span on earth,

약(藥)든 가슴으로 가야한다

얼마를 더 가면 제 잎을 잘라 가슴에 꽂아도
소리하지 않는 풀들의 무심을 배우라

it may merely be a vein on which a cabbage worm crawls.
But for thousands of names and lives to call out,
I must go with the invulnerable bosom.

How farther am I to go to learn such indifference
    as the mute grass
that does not cry out for being cut and pinned on its chest?

아름다운 사람

이 세상 아름다운 사람은 모두
제 몸 속에 아름다운 하나씩의 아이를 갖는다
사과나무가 햇볕 아래서 마침내
달고 시원한 사과를 달 듯이
이 세상 아름다운 사람은 모두
제 몸 속에 저를 닮은 하나씩의 아이를 갖는다

그들이 가꾸어 온 장롱 속의 향기들이
몰래 장롱 속을 빠져나와
잠든 그들의 머리카락과 목덜미와
목화송이 같은 아랫배로 스며들어
이 세상 아름다운 사람은
이 세상의 크기에 알맞은 하나씩의 아이를 갖는다

그들이 가꾸고 싶은 세상은
아침 숲처럼 신선한 기운으로 충만하다

그가 담그는 술은 길이 향기롭고
그의 치마는 햇볕 아래 서면
호랑나비가 되어 하늘로 날아간다
그의 어깨는 좁아도 그의 등 뒤에는 언제나
한 남자가 누울 휴식의 그늘이 드리워져 있다

A Living Soul of Beauty

Every living soul of beauty in this world
has a lovely child in his body.
Under the sunlight, as if an apple tree
bears a sweet and fresh fruit at last,
every living soul of beauty in this world
has a child resembling him in his body.

As if the perfume they have tended
in the wardrobe leaks stealthily
and infiltrates into their hair and neck
and the lower belly resembling a cotton ball,
each living soul of beauty in this world
has a child fitting to the size of this world.

The world that they wish to cultivate is filled with
fresh vitality like a forest in the morning.

The wine that he brews is aromatic for ages.
If he stands under the sun,
his skirt becomes a butterfly and flies to the sky.
Though he is narrow-shouldered, there is always a shade
behind his back in which a man can lie down to repose.

아름다운 사람은 제 몸 속의 샘물로
한 남자를 적시고
세상의 목마른 아이들을 적신다

A living soul of beauty steeps a man
in spring water within his body
and thirsty children in the world.

물 긷는 사람

새벽에 물 긷는 사람은
오늘 하루 빛나는 삶을 예비하는 사람이다

내를 건너는 바람 소리 포플러 잎에 시릴 때
아미까지 내려온 머리카락 손으로 걷어 올리며
새벽에 물 긷는 사람은
땅의 더운 피를 길어 제 삶의 정수리에
퍼붓는 사람이다

풀잎들의 귀가 우레를 예감하지 못할 때
산의 더운 혈맥에서 솟아나는
새벽의 물 긷는 사람은
흰 살이 눈부신 아침 쟁반에 제 하루를 담아
저녁의 편안을 마련하는 사람이다

나무들도 아직 이른 잠에서 깨어나지 못한
이른 새벽에
옷섶이 터질 듯 부푼 가슴을 여미며
새벽에 물 긷는 사람은
목화송이 같은 아이들과 들판 같은 남편의
하루를 예비하는 사람이다

One Who Is Drawing Water

One who draws water at daybreak is a man
who gets ready for today's dazzling life.

When the sound of the wind coming over a stream
    makes poplar leaves chilly,
tucking up hair over the eyebrows by hand,
one who draws water at daybreak is a man
who pours warm blood drawn from the ground
on the crown of his own life.

When the ears of leaves have no premonition of thunder,
one who draws water gushed from a hot blood vessel
of the mountain at daybreak is a man
who prepares for the comfort of an evening by putting
a day on the morn plate of a glaring white sunbeam.

At early daybreak
before even the trees wake up from sleep,
adjusting a upper garment to hide an ample bosom,
one who draws water is a man
who prepares a day
for cotton-ball-like children and a field-like husband.

물 긷는 사람이여, 그대 영혼의 물을 길어
마른 나뭇잎처럼 만지면 부서질 것 같은
나의 가슴에 부어다오
나는 소낙비를 맞고 가시 끝에 꽃을 다는 아카시아처럼
그대 영혼의 물을 받고 피어나는
한 송이 꽃이 되련다

One who draws water! Please draw the water out of your soul
and pour it on my bosom of fragility,
just like dry leaves.
Like an acacia flowering at its thorny tips in a shower,
I wish to be a flower blossoming
after being watered by your soul.

지상에서 부르고 싶은 노래 1

어떤 노래를 부르면 내 한 번도 바라보지 못한
짐승들이 즐거워할까
어떤 노래를 부르면 내 아직 만나지 못한
사람들도, 까치도 즐거워질까
급히 달려와 내 등 뒤에 연좌한 시간들과
노동으로 부은 소의 발등을 위해
이 세상 가장 청정한 언어를 빌어 살아있는 모든 것들의
날(日)을 노래하고 싶다
나이 들기 전에 늙어버린 단풍잎들은 내 가슴팍을 한 번 때리고
곧 땅 속으로 묻힌다
죽기 전에 나무 둥치를 감고 타오르는 저녁놀은
지상의 죽음이 저렇게 아름답다는 것을
가르치는 걸까
살이 연한 능금과 배들은 태어나 첫 번째 베어무는
어린 아이의 갓 돋은 치아의 기쁨을 위해 제 살을 바치고
군집으로 몰려오는 어둠은 제 깊은 속에다
아직 밤길에 서툰 새끼 짐승들을 위해
군데군데 별들을 박아놓았다

우리가 아무리 높이 올라도
검은 새가 나는 하늘을 밟을 수는 없고
우리가 아무리 정밀을 향해 손짓해도

Song That I Wish to Sing on Earth 1

What song makes beasts that I have never seen before
get amused?
What song makes men or even magpies
that I have never met yet get amused?
For times coming in rush, sitting behind my back
and the top of cow's swollen feet from labour,
I'd like to sing of days for all living things
in the purest words borrowed from the world.
The prematurely old maple leaves hit my chest once
and are shortly buried under the ground.
Does the blazing sundown coiling up the tree trunk
before its demise
teach that death on earth is so beautiful as such?
Apples and pears offer their tender flesh
for the delight of a child's first bite:
a gathering darkness in its deep depth
has embedded a star here and there
for clumsy cubs at night.

However high we may soar up into the air,
we cannot tread on the sky in which a black bird flies.
How much we make gesture towards precision,

정적으로 날아간 흰 나비의 길을
걸을 수는 없다
햇빛을 몰아내는 밤은 늘 기슭에서부터 몰려와
대지의 중심을 덮고
고갈되기 전에 바다에 닿아야 하는 물들은
쉬지 않고 하류로 내려간다
병들도 친숙해지면 우리의 외로움을 덮어주는
이불이 된다
산과 들판에 집 없이도 잠드는 목숨을 위해
거칠고 무딘 것들을 달래는 것이
지혜의 첫 걸음이다
달콤하지 않아도 된다, 내 부르는 노래가
발 시린 짐승의 무릎을 덮는 짚이기만 하다면,
향기롭지 않아도 된다, 내 부르는 노래가
이슬 한 방울에도 온 몸이 젖는 풀벌레의 날개를 가릴 수 있는
둥글고 넓은 나뭇잎이기만 하다면

we cannot take the road
that a white butterfly has flown into stillness.
A night driving out sunlight always descends
from the hill and covers the center of the earth:
the water that must reach the sea before being dried up
goes downstream without stopping.
If a disease is well acquainted,
it becomes a quilt covering our loneliness.
It is the first step towards wisdom to soothe
the rude and the insensible for the creatures
sleeping outdoors in the mountains and the fields.
My song need not be sweet, if it can be straw
covering the knees of beasts' cold legs.
My song need not be redolent, if it can be a wide,
    round leaf covering the wings of a grasshopper
prone to be all wet even by a dew drop.

봄밤

가난도 지나고 보면 즐거운 친구라고
배춧국 김 오르는 양은그릇들이 날을 부딪치며 속삭인다
쌀과 채소가 내 안에 타올라 목숨이 되는 것을
나무의 무언으로는 전할 수 없어 시로 써보는 봄밤
어느 집 눈썹 여린 처녀가 삼십 촉 전등 아래
이별이 긴 소설을 읽는가보다
땅 위에는 내가 아는 이름보다 훨씬 많은 사람들이
서까래 아래 제 이름 가꾸듯 제 아이를 다독여 잠재운다
여기에 우리는 한 생을 살러왔다

누가 푸른 밤이면 오리나무 숲에서 비둘기를 울리는지
동정 다는 아낙의 바느질 소리에 비둘기 울음이 기워지는 봄밤
잊혀지지 않은 것들은 모두 슬픈 빛깔을 띠고 있다
숟가락으로 되질해 온 생이 나이테 없어
이제 제 나이 헤는 것도 형벌인 세월
낫에 잘린 봄풀이 작년의 그루터기 위에
또 푸르게 돋는다
여기에 우리는 잠시 주소를 적어두러 왔다

Night in Springtime

"After poverty is gone, it becomes a jolly friend," the pieces of
nickel silverware steaming up from Chinese cabbage soup
whisper while their edges are bumping against each other.
For the fact that rice and greens flaring up in my body
turn into life cannot be conveyed by the tacitness of a tree,
I write a poem at a spring night.
Under a 30 cd light bulb, a maid with soft eyebrows
appears to read a long novel about parting.
Much more people than the names that I know on earth
put their children to sleep by patting
as if cultivating their own names under the rafts.
Here we have come to spare our life.

Who makes a dove coo in the alder woods at every blue night?
It's at a spring night that the cooing of a dove is darned
by the sounds of sewing up rents
when a housewife attaches a collar strip onto a jacket.
All that is unforgettable puts on a sad tinge.
Life measured by a spoon does not have a growth ring
and so counting my age itself is now a punishment of time.
Spring grass cut by a sickle last year sprouts again
in green on the eddish.

어느 집인들 한 오라기 근심 없는 집이 있으랴
군불 때는 연기들은 한 가정의 고통을 태우며 타오르고
근심이 쌓여 추녀가 낮아지는 집들
여기에 우리는 한줌의 삶을 기탁하러 왔다

Here, we have come to jot down our address awhile.

Is there any home that makes do without a thread of worry?
A smoke rising from the firewood heating the floor
    flares up the pain of a household,
and the eaves of houses get down by a mounted anxiety.
Here, we have come to deposit a handful of life.

햇볕이 되었거나 노을이 되었거나

들판에 흩어져 피는 꽃들에 하나하나 이름을 붙여놓은 사람들은 어언 제 이름도 꽃이 되었거나 꽃술에 취해 잠든 나비가 되었거나

한 해 봄에서 가을까지 날아가도 제 그리움까지 닿지 못한 작은 새들에 이름을 붙여준 사람들은
제 이름도 어언 새가 되었거나 오리나무 가지에서 우는 새의 울음이 되었거나

도라지꽃을 피워놓고 혼자 잠든 산과 산에 그 키와 봉우리에 알맞은 이름을 붙여놓은 사람들은
벌써 산이 되었거나 산을 씻으며 흘러가는 강물이 되었거나

산 너머 또 산 너머 잠들어 있는 마을에 제가끔 이름을 붙여준 사람들은 벌써 제 이름도 햇볕이 되었거나 햇볕의 마지막 숨소리인 노을이 되었거나

Whether It Was Either Sunlight or Sunglow

Names of those who named each of scattered flowers blooming
in the field have already become a flower or a sleeping butterfly
intoxicated by a stamen.

Names of those who named little birds flying from spring to autumn,
but unable to reach their longing, have already become a bird or
bird's cries calling amid the twigs of an alder tree.

After making a balloon flower bloom, those who fell asleep alone
in the mountains and who gave names fitting to their heights
and peaks have already become the mountains or the running
rivers bathing the mountains.

Names of those who named each village sleeping on the hill after
the hill have already become either sunlight or sundown glow,
the last breath of sunlight

산길 물길

물은 늙지 않았는데 내 머리카락만 세었다
많이 긁힌 자국이 삶이라고 가르치며
물은 자갈을 때리며 땅 끝으로 흘러간다
산길은 혼자 오르기엔 너무 넓고
햇살은 공으로 받기에는 너무 뜨겁다
아직도 헌 옷을 입고 있는 학교와 집들이,
그 속에 세든 불만의 아이들이 발목을 끌어당겨
산길은 더디다
언제나 질그릇같이 깨어지기 쉬운 나날을 보듬고
벽돌 한 장 고이고 받치며 걸어 온 길
종이를 찢어도 핏방울 듣는 날들을
이제는 고통의 선반에 올려놓고
환희의 매달처럼 바라볼 줄도 안다
습관으로 드는 숟가락이 싫지 않은 날들이
살아 있는 날이다
잊기 전에 할 일은 산과 들, 집과 거리에
이름 한 번씩 부르며 가는 일

A Mountain Pass, a Waterway

Water did not get old, but only my hair turned grey.
Telling that the vestige of a numerous scratch is life,
the water strikes pebbles and runs to the end of the earth.
A mountain pass is too wide to climb alone
and a ray of sunlight is too hot to receive for nothing.
As schools and houses still wearing old clothes
pull at the ankles of dissatisfied tenanted children,
the mountain trail is slow-footed.
Always hugging brickle days like an earthen vessel,
I've walked along the path while propping and shoring up
    a brick.
Though the paper is torn, now putting those days—
when the beads of blood are heard dropping—on a shelf of pain,
I can look at them as a medal of ecstasy.
If a spoon is not loathful to pick up habitually,
those are the days of being alive.
What should do before forgetting is to go by calling once
the name of the mountain, field, house and street.

땅 위의 이름을 사랑하네

내 천사를 흠모하지만
천사를 사랑하지 않네
하늘과 땅, 어둠과 밝음 어디에도 닿을 수 있다는
내 천사를 경외하지만
지상의 이불 소리, 숟가락 소리를 모르는
천사를 손짓하지 않네

고통이 익어 달콤한 과육이 되는 길을
상처가 익어 보석이 되는 길을 모른다면
나는 천사의 길보다 옷소매에 묻은 세월의 때를 아는
인간의 길을 택하겠네
누가 하늘의 길을 알려준다 해도
나는 지상의 한 곳에서 사과나무로 오르는
사닥다리를 놓겠네

짐승의 대(代)가 바뀌고 내 곁에서 울던 새 보이지 않고
씨앗이 죽어 다른 꽃을 땅 위로 밀어 올릴 때
바다를 건넜다 싶은 데 실개천 하나밖에 못 건넌 세월이라 해도
나는 미간의 우수, 센 머리카락
고뇌의 주름살을 사랑하겠네

I Love Names on Earth

Although I adore an angel,
I do not love him.
Although I am in awe of an angel who can get
to heaven and earth, and darkness and brightness,
I do not beckon to the angel who does not know
the rustling of a quilt and a rattling of spoons on earth.

If he does not know how pains ripen the sweet flesh of fruit
or how the wound matures itself to be a gem, I would choose
the human way recognizing the dirt of bygone years on sleeves
rather than the ways of an angel. I'll pick up the ways of man.
Although some may let me know the ways of heaven,
I'd set up a ladder to ascend an apple tree
from one place on the ground.

A generation of beasts is changed and a warbling bird near me
is not seen. When a dead seed pushes up another flower
    over the soil,
it is only a short period of time taken for crossing a rill
when I thought I have crossed over the sea.
I'd rather love melancholy between eyebrows, white hair
and the winkles of anxiety.

천사한테 내 약든 가슴, 내 아픈 체온 전할 수 없네
걸어가서 닿은 곳, 땀의 영롱을 아는 이
오직 지상에 있네
두고 떠날 집, 두고 떠날 문패 지상에 있네

나는 하늘에 있는 이름보다
땅 위의 이름을 사랑하네

I can't tell an angel of my invulnerable bosom
    as well as my sore body heat.
A place where I can reach on foot; one who knows
the brightness of sweat is only on earth.
A house and a doorplate to be left behind are on earth.

More than names in heaven
I love names on earth.

마흔 살의 동화

먹고 사는 일 걱정 되지 않으면
나는 부는 바람 따라 길 떠나겠네
가다가 찔레꽃 향기라도 스며오면
들판이든지 진흙땅이든지
그 자리에 서까래 없는 띠집을 짓겠네
거기에서 어쩌다 아지랑이 같은 여자 만나면
그 여자와 푸성귀 같은 사랑 나누겠네
푸성귀 같은 사랑 익어서
보름이고 한 달이고 같이 잠들면
나는 햇볕 아래 풀씨 같은 아이 하나 얻겠네

먹고 사는 일 걱정되지 않으면
나는 내 가진 부질없는 이름, 부질없는 조바심
흔들리는 의자, 아파트 문과 복도마다 사용되는
다섯 개의 열쇠를 버리겠네
발은 수채물에 담겨도 머리는 하늘을 향해
노래하겠네

슬픔이며 외로움이며를 말하지 않는
놀 아래 울음 남기고 죽은 노루는 아름답네
수노루 만나면 등성이서라도 새끼 배고
젖은 아랫도리 말리지 않고도

A Fairy Tale at Forty

If I were free of worry for my livelihood,
I'd go after a blowing wind.
If the scents of a wild rose smell on my way,
without caring of the field or the marsh,
I'll set up a straw-thatched cottage with no rafters.
If I come across a girl like a heat haze there,
I'll make a vegetable love with her.
If the vegetable love ripens and if we sleep together
for a fortnight or a month,
I'll have a baby just like a hayseed under the sun.

If I were free of worry for my livelihood,
I'll throw away my vain name,
anxiety, a rocking chair,
five keys to my flat doors and each corridor.
Although my feet are soused in a ditch,
I'll sing with my head up towards heaven.

Leaving cries under a sunset glow, a roe deer dying
without a word of sorrow or loneliness is beautiful.
When I meet a roebuck, I'll conceive a baby even on a ridge.
Without drying the wetted lower body,

푸른 잎 속에 스스로 뼈를 묻는
산노루 되어 나는 살겠네.

burying the bones for itself under green leaves
just like a wild roe deer, I'll live.

세상 속으로

나는 오랫동안 풀꽃의 생애를 노래해 왔다
그러나 이제는 인사에 대해서 노래하련다
이제 내 몸이 바라는 곳, 눕고 싶은 곳은
산이 아니라 물이 아니라
병이 있고 근심이 있고 자주 흰 걸레를 더럽혀야하는
마루바닥이 있는 집
여름이면 수박을 사고
월말에는 세금을 내러 은행에 가는 마을

이제 나는 이념에 물들지 않은 나무보다
이념을 구겨 호주머니에 넣을 줄 아는 사람이 좋다
선계의 산정보다 아직 청소차가 오지 않은 골목들이 좋다
등을 켜고 다가오는 별을 보면
진흙의 옷을 입은 사람들이 정겨워진다
제도가 있고 공장이 있고 못 만날 약속이 있는
집 옆에 집, 아, 사람이 살고 있다

Into the World

I have long sung of the life of flowering plants.
But from now on, I will sing of human affairs.
Now the place where my body hopes and desires
to lie down is neither on the mountains nor on water
but a house that has a disease, anxiety, and a wooden floor
making often a white rag get dirty.
It is the village where I can buy a watermelon in summer
and go to the bank to pay the monthly bills.

Now I prefer a man who knows how to crumple an ideology
into his pocket to the tree uninfected with an ideology.
I prefer a squalid alley still untouched by a garbage truck
    to the mountaintop of the taoistic land.
When I watch stars coming near with light on,
those in clay clothes become amiable to me.
There are an institution, a factory, and a house next to another
which has an appointment unable to meet. Ah, men are living.

『열하를 향하여』(1995)에서

From *Towards Jehol*

생의 노래

움 돋는 나무들은 나를 황홀하게 한다
흙 속에서 초록이 돋아나오는 걸 보면 경건해진다
삭은 처마 아래 내일 시집갈 처녀가 신부의 꿈을 꾸고
녹슨 대문 안에 햇빛처럼 밝은 아이가 잠에서 깨어난다

사람의 이름과 함께 생애를 살고
풀잎의 이름으로 시를 쓴다
세상의 것 다 녹슬었다고 핍박하는 것 아직 이르다
어느 산기슭에 샘물이 솟고
들판 가운데 풀꽃이 씨를 익힌다

절망을 두려워하는 사람들이
지레 절망을 노래하지만
누구나 마음속에 꽃잎 하나씩은 지니고 산다

근심이 비단이 되는 하루, 상처가 보석이 되는 한 해를 노래할 수 있다면
햇살의 은실 풀어 내 아는 사람에게
급박 입혀 보내고 싶다

내 열 줄 시가 아니면 무슨 말로
손수건만한 생애가 소중함을 노래하리

Song of Life

The sprouting trees hold me spellbound.
Watching greenness shoot from the soil, I feel pious.
Under rotten eaves, a maid dreams of a tomorrow's bride
and inside the rusty gate, a child as bright as sunlight wakes up.

Living life along with the name of a man,
I compose verse by the name of the leaves of grass.
Reproving all for being rusty is too early.
At the foot of a hill, spring water sprouts out
and a wild flower ripens its seeds in the field.

Although one who is in fear of despair
sings of despair beforehand,
all men each carries a petal in his bosom.

If I can sing of a day when anxiety turns into silk
    and a year when the wound turns into a jewel,
unraveling a silver thread from the sunlight
and gilding it, I wish to send it to my acquaintance.

If it is not my ten-line verse, in what words
can I sing of the pith of a handkerchief-sized life?

초록에서 숨쉬고 순금의 햇빛에서 일하는
생의 향기를 흰 종이 위에 조심히 쓰며

I write with care of the redolence of life which breathes in green and works in the pure gold sunlight on the white paper.

열하를 향하여

지원은 하룻밤에 아홉의 강을 건너
거친 모래땅 열하에 도달했다지만
나는 아홉 밤을 불면으로 지새워도 한 개의 강을 건너지 못했다
마음 덮으면 없는 강이 마음 밝히면 열의 강으로 소리를 높인다

숱 많은 머리카락 날리며 바람은 어디로 불어가는가
메마른 계절일수록 마음은 불타올라

쓰라린 시대에는 쓰라린 정신만 남는다

참말 뜨겁게 살아보리라
마음 다지면 맨살의 모래는 끓어오르지만
다가서면 열하는 마음 밖 백리에 피안으로 누워있다

아직도 멀었느냐, 아픈 발 내리고 내 몸 잠시
쉬일 곳은
네 발 디뎌 참새 발자국만한 흔적 남길 수 없는 땅 위에
낙타의 발을 이끌고 오늘도 고삐를 죄는 세월이여

어제 상수리나무 아래 쉬던 사람들
오늘은 꿈이 어지러운 그들의 적막 위에 잠들었느냐
어제 아프던 사람들, 오늘 새 살 돋은 발을 이끌고

Towards Jehol°

Although Ji-won°° is said to have crossed over nine rivers
at one night and arrived at the wild sand desert Jehol,
I could not cross over a river despite passing nine sleepless nights.
If the mind is covered up, there is no river. But if the mind is lit up,
    it raises a pitch voice of ten rivers.

With thick hair blown, where is the wind going?
The drier season comes, the more fiery the mind is.

In a bitter epoch, a poignant spirit stays.

Truly, I will live avidly as I can.
When the mind is hardened, the sand of naked flesh boils up.
Drawing near to Jehol, it lies in another world
    beyond one hundred-ri from the mind.

Is it still far away? —the place where I can take rest
for a while to relieve the pain of my feet.
On the ground where even four feet cannot leave a trace of
    sparrow's footprints,
the passing of time steers the camel's feet
    and tightens up its rein even today!

고원을 건넜느냐

바라보면 눈물겨운 것들 너무 많아
내 작은 가슴으로 그것들의 아픈 꿈 다 끌어안을 수 없지만
눈물의 값짐을 아는 자만이 사랑의 귀함도 알 수 있다

가자, 날 저물면 처마 아래 들고 날 밝으면 모래밭을 걸어
슬프고 작은 것 불러 모아 그들의 등 다독이며 가자
고독도 손잡으면 친구이리니
마음의 거친 물결 재우며 가자

Those who rested yesterday under the oak tree are sleeping
over their quietude in a today's troubled dream?

Those who were sick yesterday have crossed over the highlands
while leading their proud flesh feet today?

When I look around, there are so many things pathetic.
Though I can't hug all of their painful dreams with my small chest,
those who know the value of tears only know the value of love.

Let's go. When the sun goes down, let's stay under the eaves:
　when the day beaks, let's walk on the sands after calling
together those who are sad and small while petting their backs.
When solitude is joined in hands, it becomes a friend.
Let's go on while putting the raging waves of mind to sleep.

° Jehol or Rehe is a prefecture-level city in Hebei province, situated northeast of Beijing. It is best known as the site of the Mountain Resort, a vast imperial garden and palace formerly used by the Qing emperors as summer residence.

°° At 44, Park Ji-won (1737~1805) joined the Joseon envoy to Chinese emperor who stayed in the summer palace in Jehol in 1780. After his return from Jehol, he wrote the book entitled *The Jehol Diary*.

서풍에 기대어 1

별리만큼 아름다운 것은 없다.
간 이파리 하나쯤 떼어 가는 아픔이야
별리의 아름다움에 비길 수 있으랴

마음보다 치장이 아름다운 서풍이여
너의 안식의 기도 앞에서 몇 사람은 저녁 수저를 들고
몇 사람은 길 위에서 이슬처럼 깨어지기 쉬운 약속을 한다.
저녁으로 갈수록 사람과 사람 사이
모든 언약들이 반짝인다.

우리는 이제 이른 저녁을 먹고
들 가운데 서서 오늘보다 아름다운 내일을 말할 차례다
양치기 소년들의 고단한 발을 쉬게 하고
펄럭이는 내일의 치맛자락을 끌어당기며
만남보다 진한 이별을 말할 차례다
아무도 시키지 않았는데
문 밖에서 바람은 흰 피륙을 짜고 있다
사람의 하루가 고단하여 침실에 몸을 누이는 저녁에도
과일 나무의 과일은 저 혼자 익는다

서쪽으로 가면 웬일인지 하늘로 오르는 사닥다리가 있을 것 같아
오늘도 들판 끝을 헤매다 서풍의 옷자락에 싸여 돌아온다

Standing against the West Wind 1

Nothing is more beautiful than parting.
The pain of cutting out a lobe of the liver
may bear comparison with the beauty of a parting.

A west wind, your finery is more beautiful than mind.
Before your sabbatical prayer, some lift spoons and chopsticks
and others make promise as fragile as a dewdrop on the path.
As an evening comes nearer, all of the vows made
    among men sparkle.

After having an early supper and standing amid the field, now
we have our turn to speak of tomorrow, more beautiful than today.
Letting the worn-out foot of a shepherd take rest
and pulling the flapping long skirt of tomorrow, we have our turn
to speak of rather an exquisite parting than a meeting.
Although no one told the wind,
it weaves white fabric outside near the door.
In the evening when a man lies down in his bedroom
for a day's fatigue, the fruit ripens on the tree by itself.

If I go westward, there is likely to be a ladder ascending to heaven.
Lingering around the edge of the field, I, wrapped by the hem

先史로 돌아가고 싶은 장엄한 몸짓인 서풍이여
너의 치마 끝에 내리는 놀의 물감으로
오늘 우리는 주홍빛 이별을 기록해야 한다

될 수만 있으면 바위에 기록하리라
어둠 뒤에서 마지막 한 겹 속옷마저 벗고
알몸으로 초록 위를 부는 서풍이여
이맘때쯤 바람과 능금나무의 화간에도
우리는 박수 치리
그리고 세상의 푸름들이 시들기 전에
우리는 필생의 편지를 한 사람의 이름 앞으로 보내야 하리

of the west wind, return.
The west wind, a majestic gesture desiring to return to prehistory!
With the colour of a sunset glow falling on the hem of your skirt,
we have to record a vermilion parting today.

If possible, I will put it down on the rock.
Undressing the last underclothing behind the darkness,
in its naked body blows over the green the west wind!
At this time of the year, I will clap even for the fornication
between the wind and the crab.
Before the greenness of the world wilts away,
we ought to post a letter of our lifetime to the name of a man.

마음 속 푸른 이름

아직 이르구나
내 이 지상의 햇빛, 지상의 바람 녹슬었다고 슬퍼하는 것은,
아직 이르구나, 내 사람들의 마음 모두
잿빛이 되었다고 탄식하는 것은
수평으로 나는 흰 새의 날개에 내려앉는
저 모본단 같은 구름장과
우단 같은 바람 앞에 제 키를 세우는 상수리나무들
꿈꾸는 유리 강물, 햇볕 한 움큼씩 베어 문 나생이 잎새들
마음 열고 바라보면 아직도 이 세상 늙지 않아
외출할 때 돌아와 부를 노래만은
언제나 문고리에 매어둔다

이제 조그맣게 속삭여도 되리라
내일 아침에는 이 봄에 못 피었던 수제비꽃 한 송이
길 옆에 피고
수제비꽃 옆에 어제까지 없던 우체국이 하나
새로 지어질 것이라고,
내 귓속말로 전해도 되리라
오늘 태어나는 아이가 내일 아침에는 주홍신을 신고
마음 속 가장 따뜻한 말을 싸서 부치러
우체국으로 갈 것이라고

The Blue Name in Mind

It's still early for me
to grieve over the rustiness of sunlight and wind on the ground.
It's still early for me to lament that the minds of my people
have all turned into grey.
Before a sheet of Chinese silk-like cloud and the velvet-like wind
descending on the wings of a white bird flying horizontally,
the oak trees erect their height upright.
The dreamy glass river and the leaves of shepherd's purse
    biting a mouthful of sunlight—
when I behold with the open mind, this world is not old yet.
When I go out, I always tie a song to the doorknob to sing
on my return.

Now, it may be all right to whisper low:
"Tomorrow morning, a violet which did not bloom this spring
will bloom by a track
and a postoffice which was not there by the violet
will be newly built."
These words will be delivered in my whispering:
"A baby born today will put on the scarlet shoes tomorrow
morning and go to send the warmest, wrapped words
from the heart at the postoffice."

작은 이름 하나라도

이 세상 작은 이름 하나라도
마음 끝에 닿으면 등불이 된다
아플 만큼 아파 본 사람만이
망각과 폐허도 가꿀 줄 안다

내 한 때 너무 멀어서 못 만난 허무
너무 낯설어 가까이 못 간 이념도
이제는 푸성귀 잎에 내리는 이슬처럼
불빛에 씻어 손바닥 위에 얹는다

세상은 적이 아니라고,
고통도 쓰다듬으면 보석이 된다고
나는 얼마나 오래 악보 없는 노래로 불러왔던가

이 세상 가장 여린 것, 가장 작은 것
이름만 불러도 눈물겨운 것
그들이 내 친구라고
나는 얼마나 오래 여린 말로 노래했던가

내 걸어갈 동안은 세상은 나의 벗
내 수첩에 기록되어 있는 모음이 아름다운 사람의 이름들
그들 위해 나는 오늘도 한 술 밥, 한 쌍 수저

Even If a Little Name

Even if a little name in the world touches a tip of mind,
it becomes a lamp.
Only those who had as much pain as they could
know how to take care of oblivion and ruin.

Nothingness was once too far for me to meet
and ideologies were too unfamiliar to go near.
Now like a falling dew on the leaves of greens,
I put them on my palm after washing in light.

"The world is not an enemy,
and if caressed, suffering becomes a jewel,"
how long have I recited as a song without a score?

"A thing tenderest, tiniest
and a thing pathetic when called by its name only;
they are my friends,"
how long have I sung of them in the soft words?

The world is my friend while I'm walking on.
The names of those whose vowels in names are pretty in my jotter—
for them, I set a spoonful of rice, a spoon and a pair of chopsticks

식탁 위에 올린다

잊혀지면 안식이 되고
마음 끝에 닿으면 등불이 되는
이 세상 작은 이름 하나를 위해
내 쌀 씻어 놀 같은 저녁밥 지으며

on the dining table.

If forgotten, the name will rest in peace:
if touched at the tip of mind, it will be a lamp.
For a little name in this world,
I wash rice and cook it for supper like a glow of sundown.

『유리의 나날』(1998)에서

From *Days of Glass*

유리, 노래

그것은 말이 끝난 다음에 남겨둘 말
그것은 마지막 페이지 다음에 넘길 책장
그것은 이별 뒤에 오는 해후
그것은 노래가 그친 뒤에 부를 노래

내 안에서 움돋는 유리여

그것은 모든 사랑이 식은 뒤에 사랑할 가슴
그것은 죽은 들판에 다시 돋는 잎

Glass, A Song

That's a word to be left after a speech.
That's a book leaf to be turned over after the last one.
That's a chance meeting after parting.
That's a song to be sung after the end of singing.

Glass, you are budding out within me!

That's a heart to love after all the love turns cool.
That's a new leaf budding up again from the dead field.

유리에 닿는 길 1

오척 단구를 용광로에 담그고
모발이 타고 살이 불붙는 소리를 들어라
물의 몸이 사라지고
뼈들이 몸 밖으로 빠져나가는 소리를 들어라
아무리 번쩍이는 날빛이라도
그것이 칠흑의 어둠 속에서 태어난 것이 아니면
광휘일 수 없다
아무리 고혹의 향기일지라도
그것이 매운 바람과 모진 추위를 이기고 온 것이 아니면
향기일 수 없다
저 염열과 갈증의 날들을 지나서 공허 뒤에 세우는
과육의 나라처럼
끓는 쇳물 뒤에 고요로 눕는 장검의 사슬처럼
찬란한 것은 모두 어둠 뒤에 있다

몸이 아는 불의 뜨거움, 몸이 아는 얼음의 차가움도
벗어놓고
가시에 찢기고 바늘에 찔려도 아프지 않은 마음으로
세상의 벼랑길 걸어갈 수 있다면
그때 비로소 나는
상처마저도 사랑한 삶을 살았다고 하리
수천의 기왓장으로 무성하던 잎새들

A Pathway to Glass 1

Put a five-cheok° short stature in a furnace
and hear the noise of burning hair and flesh.
When water from the body disappears,
hear the noise of bones slipping out of the body.
However bright the daylight is,
if not born out of pitch darkness,
it cannot be radiant.
However captivating the scent is,
if not beat the biting wind and cold,
it is not a redolence.
Like a fruit-flesh country set up
after a void in the wake of torrid and thirsty days
or like the sharp edge of a long sword lying down
    in silence after a molten metal,
all that is glittering lies behind darkness.

Throwing off a heat of fire and an icy coldness
of which the body is aware,
despite being torn off by a thorn and pierced by a needle,
if I can walk on the bluff of the world with a painless mind,
then, I'd say at last
I have lived life that I loved even scars.

땅으로 내려놓고
혼자 겨울을 버티는 나무처럼
모든 죄질들이 몸 밖으로 빠져나가고 나면
그때 내 생은
유리의 문전에 들었다고 하리

내 생애 단 한 번 불러보고 싶은 순수에게 신앙으로 바칠
내 마음의 유리,
정신의 보석

Putting down the thousands tiles of lush leaves
on the ground
like a tree enduring winter by itself,
when all of the sinful nature gets out of my body,
then, I'd say
my life is admitted to a gate of glass.

Only once in my life, I wish to call out purity
and to dedicate a glass of my mind,
a gem of my spirit, to purity as a faith.

° *Cheok* is a Korean unit of measuring length. One cheok is equivalent to 30.3cm. Only once in my life, I wish to call out purity and to dedicate a glass of my mind, a gem of my spirit, to purity as a faith.

유리의 나날 1

내 쌀과 물의 끼니 버리고 한 하늘 거뜬히 바위로 설 수 있다면
긴 배고픔과 현란한 식사의 유혹을 버리고
뼈 속까지 명징한 유리의 날을 맞을 수 있으리

내 솜과 모직의 옷을 버리고 한 계절 가득 푸른 나무로 설 수 있다면
염열과 냉혹의 시련 이기고 뿌리 하나로 세상 견디는
핏줄까지 청정한 유리의 날을 맞을 수 있으리

풍진 세월 끌고 가는 물의 몸이여
금욕과 인종 두려워하는 사금파리 마음이여
돌아보아 등 뒤에 쌓인 먼지의 날에 발이 묶여
아직도 수정의 내일 앞에 나는 넉넉히 이르지 못하는 구나

낙타의 등같이 나를 휘게 한 노역은
아직도 단백의 발등 위에 철근의 집을 짓지만
이녕 진창, 걸어온 세상길에서도
바람처럼 세사에 표연할 수 있다면
내 고단한 하루, 유혹의 잔을 뿌리치고
증류수 같이 순연한 유리의 날을 맞을 수 있으리

Days of Glass 1

If I can dump a daily meal made of rice and water,
    stand easily in the sky as on the rock,
and resist a lure of long hunger and a fabulous meal,
I'll meet the days of glass lucid up to the bones.

If I can give up cotton or wool clothes
    and stand as a green tree in a full season,
defeating an ordeal of torridity and cruelty,
    and enduring the world with one root,
I'll meet the days of glass pure to the vein of blood.

What a water body dragging a wind-blown dusty time!
What a mind in fear of abstinence and endurance
    like a broken piece of chinaware!
Looking back, I see my feet tied to the day of dust
    heaped behind my back and yet I have not arrived fully
before tomorrow's crystal.

Although labor has made me crooked like a camel's back
and still sets up a steel house on top of a protein foot,
on the muddy road as well as on the worldly road,
if I'm casual about worldly affairs like a wind,

타고 나면 재가 되고 말 욕망이여
내 한 즈믄 날 너를 버리고
뇌우 끝에 열리는 푸른 하늘같은 오전을 만날 수 있다면
한 생애 넉넉히 유리로 견딜 수 있으리

내 몸, 이슬 한 방울로 전신을 적시는 나뭇잎이기만 하다면
내 마음, 천년 함묵에도 외롭지 않은 바위이기만 하다면

then shaking off my weary day and the glass of temptation,
I can meet the day of pure glass like the distilled water.

Desire is nothing but ashes after being burnt down!
Forsaking my thousand days,
if I can meet the morning like the blue sky opening
after a thunderstorm, a lifetime will be sustained enough as glass.

If my body is a leaf of tree soaked fully by a dewdrop
and if my mind is not a lonely rock despite a thousand years' silence

유리의 나날 9

—부석사에서

극락세계는 유리로 되어있다고
아미타경은 목판의 얼굴을 들어 나에게 가르치지만
나무처럼 옷벗어도 부끄럽지 않은 자만이 극락에 들 수 있다고
유동나무 잎새가 내 발 등에 떨어지며 나를 꾸짖는다

발가락 하나까지 헝겊으로 가린 내 몸이
유리의 투명에 이르기 위해서는
즈믄 날 나무의 발치에 무릎 꿇을 줄 알아야 한다.

내 안에 유리는 없고
내 마신 수정의 물도 검은 체액이 되는 것은
내 몸보다 더 큰 욕망 때문일까
풀벌레 울음 속에서 욕망 한 가닥 가위로 잘라내다
누더기 욕망 어디에 가위를 대야 할지 몰라
옷섶만 자른다

정토가 어디 있느냐고 바람이 물으면
운판의 구름 갈기가 하늘을 가리킨다
누가 물의 몸으로 하늘에 오르겠는가
바람과 구름의 질타에도 황홀해질 때가 되면
발이 수렁에 있어도 거기가 정토라 하리

Days of Glass 9

—At Buseoksa

Although the Amitabha sutra, lifting its face of woodblock
scriptures, teaches me that paradise is made of glass,
only the unbashful one like a naked tree can enter paradise;
a leaf of tung oil tree falling on top of my foot chides me.

To get to the lucency of glass with my body draped in patches
down to the toes, I should know how to kneel down
at the foot of a tree for a thousand days.

There is no glass within my body.
The crystal water that I drink turns into black secretion
because I have a greater desire than my body?
Cutting off a strand of desire with scissors amidst
    the chirping of insects from the grass,
simply, I cut off the gusset
without knowing where to cut the tattered desire.

If the wind asks where the pure land is,
the maned clouds on a buddhist gong° point to the sky.
Who can ascend the sky with the body of water?
When I'm ecstatic despite the rebuke of the winds and clouds,

새는 하늘에 없는 길을 내는데
나는 산중에 있는 길마저 놓친다
마음의 남루 씻기 전에는 아미타에 들 수 없다고
고색창연한 무량수전이 내 등을 떠민다

I'd say that's the pure land even if my feet are in mud.

Birds beat a path which is absent in the sky,
but I lose even my pathway on the mountains.
"Before cleaning up a meanness of your mind",
the time-honoured Muryangsujeon[○○] saying, "You cannot
enter the land of Amitabha", pushes me out.

[○] A cloud-shaped Buddhist gong: one of the four Buddhist altar objects often hung together in the bell tower. The other three are the drum, the Buddhist bell, and the fish-shaped wooden gong.

[○○] A hall in a temple that enshrines the statue of Amitabha Buddha at Buseoksa

유리에 묻는다

나는 언제 피는 꽃처럼 육체를 향기로 가득 채울 수 있을 것인가

나는 언제 계절처럼 찬란하게 옷 갈아입을 수 있을 것인가

높은 곳으로는 못 올라가는 시냇물처럼
나는 언제 바닥이 더 즐거운 물의 마음이 될 것인가

나는 언제 살 속에 집을 짓고 수정의 영혼을 그 안에 앉힐 수 있을 것인가

나는 언제 해골의 물을 마시고 하룻밤 사이에 득도할 수 있을 것인가

내 문득 유리에 닿는 날
나는 모든 병자들에게 입 맞추고 거지에 무릎 꿇을 수 있을 것인가

나는 언제 한 개의 삽으로 남산을 옮길 수 있을 것인가

나는 다만 하나의 시인으로
풀잎처럼 세상 가운데 흔들리며 흔들리며 저물 것인가

An Inquiry Is Made to Glass

When can I fill my body with redolence like a blooming flower?

When can I change my clothes floridly like a season?

Like a brook that cannot go upstream to a high place,
when can I have a mind of water preferring its bottom?

When can I set up a house in the flesh and enshrine
a crystal soul in it?

When can I obtain enlightenment overnight after drinking water
from the skull?°

On the day when I arrive at glass all of sudden,
can I kiss all of the sick and kneel down before the begger?

When can I move Mt. Namsan with a shovel?

Simply as one of the poets, shall I'll vanish into dusk
while waving and waving in the world like the leaves of grass?

° On his way to T'ang China for study, the great Buddhist monk Wonhyo (617-686) who lived during the later Silla kingdom is known to have obtained enlightenment overnight after drinking water from the skull.

내 안의 유리

이 세상엔 한없는 것도 있다
갈망 없이도 무한한 것이 세상에는 있다
저 뭉게구름의 속살 같은 것
차원을 건너다니는 바람의 치맛자락 같은 것

풀잎의 마음이라면 저 고요에 닿을 수 있다
천 길 땅 속에서 길어 올린 샘물의 마음이라면
저 순수에 닿을 수 있다

화강암 편마암만 견고한 것이 아니다
몸을 받친 뼈 아니라도 세상엔 견고한 것이 또 있다
풀잎의 고요, 샘물의 순수를 껴안은 마음이야 또한
얼마나 견고한가

유리여, 어떤 불꽃으로 태워도
너의 투명한 육신 검은 재가 되지 않는다
어떤 혹한에도 너의 명징한 육신 얼음이 되지 않는다
순수에 길든 너의 몸은 깨어져 천 조각 파편으로 흩어질지언정
먹빛 진창에 살 섞지 않는다
추위에는 적과 같이 완강하고 더위에는 얼음같이 냉혹한 고절에
한서(寒暑)를 두려워하는 내 몸 다가가지 못한다

Glass inside Me

There is a thing that has no bounds in the world.
Even though no desiring, there is a thing infinite.
Something like the inner flesh of cumuliform.
Something like a skirt of the wind crossing dimensions.

The mind of a grass leaf can arrive at that quietude.
If it is the mind of spring water drawn deep down from the earth,
it can arrive at that purity.

What is solid is neither granite nor gneiss only.
Besides the bones sustaining a body, there is another thing
    solid in he world.
The quietude of grass; how solid is the mind
holding the purity of spring water!

Glass, whatever fire is set on you,
your crystal body does not turn into black ashes.
By any bitter cold spell, your lucid body does not turn into ice.
Although your body tamed by purity may be scattered into
a thousand broken pieces, the flesh does not mix with the black mud.
My body either in fear of cold or heat does not go near a lofty virtue
—obstinate in cold like an enemy and callous in heat like an ice.

모든 향기와 고혹의 향연을 베어버리면
너의 지순至純과 고절에 내 도달할 수 있을까
마음 가운데 짓는 욕망의 집들을 천인의 절벽 끝으로 밀어던지면
너의 지고와 초탈에 내 이를 수 있을까

세속엔 단호하고 정결에는 관대한 유리여
그러나 끼니에 노복이고 주림에 맹목인 내 몸
즈믄 날의 절식으로도 너에게 도달할 수 없다
다만 무릎 꿇어 너의 앞에 절할 뿐

If I cut off all kinds of fragrance or riveting feasts,
can I reach your purity as well as the lofty virtue?
If I cast the cells of desire built in my mind off a bottomless bluff,
can I get to your sublimity or transcendence?

Glass, how stern you are to the world and how generous to purity!
But my body is an old thrall to a meal and blind to hunger.
I cannot even get to you by fasting for a thousand days.
What I can do is simply to kneel down and to bow before you.

유리, 마을

—석리라는 곳

세상에서 가장 아름다운 곳, 석리라는 곳
그곳엔, 여름엔 장다리꽃 피고
겨울엔 마른 수숫대 위로 싸락눈 온다

세상 사람들 아무도 그곳을 몰라도
나와 가재와 다람쥐는 그곳을 안다

꽃진 그루터기마다 볕살이 와서 한시름 놀다 가고
아무도 바라보지 않는데
메밀꽃 제 신명에 하얗게 핀다

말벌들은 제 먹을 양식보다 훨씬 많은 꿀을 모으느라
한낮이 분주하고
밤이면 아직 이름 불려지지 않은 별들이
산마루에 돋는 곳

세상 사람들 아무도 그곳을 몰라도
나와 말똥구리와 굴뚝새는 그곳을 안다

Glass, A Village

—The Place Called Seok-ri

A most beautiful spot in the world—that's Seokri.
There, a stalk of radishes blooms in summer
and snow fellets fall down in winter over dried sorghum stalks.

Although no one knows of its whereabout,
a crayfish, a squirrel and I know where it is.

The sunbeam comes down to each stubble of fallen flowers
 and departs after having a fun to release anxiety.
Although no one looks at buckwheat,
it blooms exhilaratingly in white by itself.

Wasps are busy at noon with gathering honey
more than they can eat.
At night, that's where unnamed stars are rising
over the ridge of a mountain.

Although no one knows of where the place is,
a tumblebug, a wren and I know where it is.

유리의 길 3

개미를 보면 나는 너무 멀리까지 와버렸다는 생각이 든다
나비를 보면 나는 너무 많은 악에 길들었다는 생각이 든다
잔디를 보면, 냉이꽃을 보면 나는 너무 많은 봄을 놓쳐버렸다는 생각이 든다

나생이 둥글레꽃 꽃다지 민들레
고사리 우엉잎 도꼬마리 이질풀
아, 나는 너무 많은 이름들을 놓쳐버렸다

구름을 보면 나는 아직도 내 앞에 걸어가야 할 길이
많이 남았다는 생각이 든다
강물을 보면, 파도를 보면 나는 아직도 내 앞에 출렁일 것이 많이 남았다는 생각이 든다

A Pathway to Glass 3

Looking at an ant, methinks, I have come too far.
Looking at a butterfly, methinks, I'm accustomed to
too many evils.
Looking at grass and the flower of shepherd's purce,
I have missed so many seasons of spring, methinks.

Shepherd's purse, Solomon's seal, whitlow grass, dandelion,
bracken, burdock leaf, cocklebur, and cranesbill.
Ah, I missed so many names.

Looking at the clouds, I have still many miles to walk on
before me, methinks.
Looking at the river and the waves, I have still many things
left to roll before me, methinks.

『내가 만난 사람은 모두 아름다웠다』(2000)에서

From *Those Whom I Have Met Were All Beautiful*

내가 만난 사람은 모두 아름다웠다

잎 넓은 저녁으로 가기 위해서는
이웃들이 더 따뜻해져야 한다
초승달을 데리고 온 밤이 우체부처럼
대문을 두드리는 소릴 듣기 위해서는
채소처럼 푸른 손으로 하루를 씻어놓아야 한다
이 세상에 살고 싶어서 별을 쳐다보고
이 세상에 살고 싶어서 별 같은 약속도 한다
이슬 속으로 어둠이 걸어 들어갈 때
하루는 또 한 번의 작별이 된다
꽃송이가 뚝뚝 떨어지며 완성하는 이별
그런 이별은 숭고하다
사람들의 이별도 저러할 때
하루는 들판처럼 부유하고
한 해는 강물처럼 넉넉하다
내가 읽은 책은 모두 아름다웠다
내가 만난 사람도 모두 아름다웠다
나는 낙화만큼 희고 깨끗한 발로
하루를 건너가고 싶다
떨어져서도 아름다운 꽃잎의 말로
내 아는 사람에게
상추 잎 같은 편지를 보내고 싶다

Those Whom I have Met Were All Beautiful

In order to get into a broadleaf evening,
the neighbours ought to be more warm-hearted.
Like a postman, the night fetching the crescent moon
to hear knocking on a door should clean up a day
like a vegetable with green hands.
Craving for living in this world, one looks up at stars:
craving for living in this world, one makes a star-like vow.
When the darkness walks into dews,
a day bids a farewell once more.
A farewell consummated by the falling flowers—
such a farewell is noble.
If man's parting is made like that,
a day becomes fertile like the field
and a year gets affluent like the river.
The books that I've read were all beautiful.
Those whom I've ever met were all beautiful, too.
With a white, clean foot like a fallen flower,
I wish to cross over a day.
Though fallen, in the words of beautiful petals
I wish to send a lettuce-like letter
to my acquaintance.

풀잎

초록은 초록만으로 이 세상을 적시고 싶어 한다
작은 것은 아름다워서
비어 있는 세상 한 켠에 등불로 걸린다
아침보다 더 겸허해지려고 낯을 씻는 풀잎
순결에는 아직도 눈물의 체온이 배어있다
배추 값이 폭등해도 풀들은 제 키를 줄이지 않는다
그것이 풀들의 희망이고 생애이다
들 가운데 사과가 익고 있을 때
내 사랑하는 사람은 자기만의 영혼을 이끌고
어느 불 켜진 집에 도착했을까
하늘에서 별똥별 떨어질 때
땅에서는 풀잎 하나와 초록 숨 쉬는
갓난아기 하나 태어난다
밤새 아픈 꿈꾸고도 새가 되어 날아오르지 못하는
내 이웃들
그러나 누가 저 풀잎 앞에서 짐짓
슬픈 내일을 말할 수 있는가
사람들이 따뜻한 방을 그리워할 때
풀들은 따뜻한 흙을 그리워한다

Leaves of Grass

Green wishes to colour the world with green only.
Since a small thing is beautiful,
it is hung as a lantern in an empty space of the world.
The leaves of grass wash their faces to look humbler
    than they are in the morning.
In purity, the temperature of tears is still embedded.
Though the price of Chinese cabbage rises sharply,
the grass does not shorten its height;
that is a hope and a life of grass.
While apples are ripening in the field,
has my sweetheart led her own soul
and arrived at a lighted house?
When a shooting star falls from the sky,
a leaf of grass and a baby drawing a green breath
are born on earth.
My neighbours,
they dream a painful dream all night long,
    but cannot fly up as a bird.
But who can speak of a sad tomorrow deliberately
before the grass?
When people long for a warm room,
the grass misses the warm soil.

언제 삶이 위기 아닌 적이 있었던가

언제 삶이 위기 아닌 적이 있었던가
껴입을수록 추워지는 것은 시간과 세월뿐이다
돌의 냉혹, 바람의 칼날, 그것이 삶의 내용이거니
생의 질량 속에 발을 담그면
몸 전체가 잠기는 이 숨막힘
설탕 한 숟갈의 회유에도 글썽이는 날은
이미 내가 잔혹 앞에 무릎 꿇은 날이다
슬픔이 언제 신음소릴 낸 적 있었던가
고통이 언제 뼈를 드러낸 적 있었던가
목조계단처럼 쿵쿵거리는, 이미 내 친구가 된 고통들
그러나 결코 위기가 우리를 패망시키지는 못한다
내려칠수록 날카로워지는 대장간의 쇠처럼
매질은 따가울수록 생을 단련시키는 채찍이 된다
이것은 결코 수식이 아니니
고통이 끼니라고 말하는 나를 욕하지 말라
누군들 근심의 힘으로 밥 먹고
수심의 디딤돌을 딛고 생을 건너간다
아무도 보료 위에 누워 위기를 말하지 말라
위기의 삶만이 꽃피는 삶이므로

Hasn't There Ever Been Life without a Crisis?

Hasn't there ever been life without a crisis?
What is colder in more clothes on; that's time
  and the passing of time only.
The callousness of a stone or the knife blade of the wind;
  that's the contents of life.
If I put my foot into a mass of life,
this stuffiness chokes me as if my whole body were sunken.
If tears gather by the placation of spoonful sugar,
it is the day when I have already knelt down before atrocity.
Has sadness ever moaned?
Has pain ever exposed bones?
Like a thudding wooden staircase, the pain has already
  become my friend
but a crisis does never beat us.
Like iron that grows sharper by the beating of a blacksmith,
a harsher flogging changes to a whip that disciplines life.
This is never an emblazonment at all;
don't abuse me when I say that pain is a meal.
Everyone has a meal by dint of anxiety
and crosses over life by stamping on the steppingstone of
  a deep anxiety.
Don't speak of a crisis while lying down on a fancy mattress,
for the life of a crisis is only a life of blossoming.

시

성공하려고 시를 쓴 건 아니다
물살같이 아려오는 것 있어 시를 썼다
출세하려고 시를 쓴 건 아니다
슬픔이 가슴을 앨 때 그 슬픔 달래려고
시를 썼다
내 이제 시를 쓴 지 삼십년
돌아보면 돌밭과 자갈밭에 뿌린 눈물 흔적
지워지지 않고 있지만
나는 눈물을 이슬처럼 쓰다듬으며 걸어왔다
발등에 찬 눈 흩날려도
잃어버린 것의 이름 불러 등을 토닥이며 걸어왔다
읽은 책이 모두 별이 되는 것은 아니었다
지식이란 부스럼투성이의 노인에 다가가는 것
앎은 오히려 저문 들판처럼 나를 어둠으로 몰고 갔으니

그러나 노래처럼 나를 불러주는 것
이기는 일보다 지는 일이 더 아름다움을
깨우쳐 준 것은 시뿐이다
나무처럼 내 물음에 손 흔들어주는 것은
시뿐이다
고요의 힘인, 삶의 탕약인

Poetry

It's not true for me to have written poetry to succeed in life.
I have written poetry because there was something stinging
like a water current.
I did not write poetry to advance in the world.
When my heart sickens for sadness, I wrote poetry
to soothe a heartrending grief.
Now thirty years have passed since I began to write poetry.
Looking back, the trace of tears scattered on the stone
and in the gravelly field has not been effaced though,
I've walked along, caressing tears as if a dewdrop.
When the top of my feet is strewn with the cold snow,
I've come calling names of things lost and patted their backs.
All of the books that I have read did not turn to stars.
Knowledge is something that goes near a blotchy old man
since knowing, like the dusky field, has only led me to the darkness.

Yet like a song, something calling out and enlightening me
that losing is more beautiful than winning;
that's just poetry.
Like a tree, waving its hand to my inquiry
is just poetry;
the strength of silence, the herbal decoction of life.

돌에 대해서

구르는 것이 일생인 삶도 있다
구르다가 마침내 가루가 되는 삶도 있다
가루가 되지 않고는 온몸으로 사랑했다고 말할 수 없으리라
뜨겁게 살 수 있는 길이야 알몸밖에 더 있느냐
알몸으로 굴러가서 기어코 핏빛 사랑 한번 할 수 있는 것이야
맨살밖에 더 있느냐
맨살로 굴러가도 아프지 않은 게
돌멩이밖에 더 있느냐
이 세상 모든 것 기다리다 지친다 했는데
기다려도 기다려도 지치지 않는 게 돌 밖에 더 있느냐

빛나는 생이란 높은 데 있는 것이 아니다
가장 치열한 삶은 가장 낮은 데 있다고
깨어져서야 비로소 삶을 완성하는
돌은 말한다
구르면서 더욱 단단해지는 삶이,
작아질수록 더욱 견고해지는 삶이 뿌리 가까이 있다고
깨어지면서 더욱 뭉쳐지는 돌은 말한다

Of a Stone

There is a life of living that is rolling.
At last, there is life turning into dust after rolling.
If not turn into dust, it can't be said to have loved
  with a whole body.
Is there any other way to live in flame but being naked?
After rolling in a naked body, is there any other way
but being naked to make a bloody love possible after all?
Even if it rolls in nakedness, is there any other thing
but a stone that does not feel painful?
Everything in the world is said to get tired in waiting,
what else is there but a stone untiring in waiting after waiting?

A glittering life is not at the top of the pile
but a most intense life is at the bottom;
consummating its life by being broken at last,
the stone says.
Life gets harder in rolling—
the smaller the stone is, the harder life is near to the root.
Turning into a harder mass by being broken, says the stone.

별까지는 가야한다

우리 삶이 먼 여정일지라도
걷고 걸어 마침내 하늘까지는 가야한다
닳은 신발 끝에 노래를 달고
걷고 걸어 마침내 별까지는 가야한다

우리가 걷는 마을엔 잎새들 푸르고
꽃은 칭찬하지 않아도 향기로 핀다
숲과 나무에 깃들인 삶들은 아무리 노래해도
목쉬지 않는다
사람의 이름이 가슴으로 들어와 마침내
꽃이 되는 걸 아는 데
나는 쉰 해를 보냈다
미움도 보듬으면 노래가 되는 걸 아는 데
나는 반생을 보냈다

나는 너무 오래 햇볕을 만졌다
이제 햇볕을 뒤로 하고 어둠 속으로 걸어가
별을 만져야한다
나뭇잎이 짜 늘인 그늘이 넓어
마침내 그것이 천국이 되는 것을
나는 이제 배워야 한다

Up to the Stars Must We Go

Although our life is a long journey,
we must walk on up to the sky at last.
Hanging a song at the tip of worn shoes,
we must walk on up to the stars at last.

In the village where we walk, leaves are green
and flowers bloom in redolence without a praise.
No matter how long dwellers in the woods or trees sing,
their voices do not get hoarse.
I have spent fifty years to realize
that the name of a man coming into my bosom
becomes a flower at last.
I have spent a half of my life to realize
that even hatred can be a song if hugged.

I have touched the sunbeam too long.
Now leaving the sunbeam behind, I must walk into the darkness
to touch the stars.
Now I must learn that a bower woven by foliage
is broadly stretched
and that at last it turns into heaven.

먼지의 세간들이 일어서는 골목을 지나
성사가 치러지는 교회를 지나
빛이 쌓이는 사원을 지나
마침내 어둠을 밝히는 별까지는
나는 걸어서 걸어서 가야 한다

Passing through the dusty lane of a mundane life,
passing by a church in which a sacred rite is held,
passing by a temple on which light is heaped up,
and at last to the stars which illuminate the darkness,
I must walk and walk along on foot.

벚꽃 그늘에 앉아 보렴

벚꽃 그늘 아래 잠시 생애를 벗어놓아 보렴
입던 옷 신던 신발 벗어놓고
누구의 아비 누구의 남편도 벗어놓고
햇살처럼 쨍쨍한 맨몸으로 앉아보렴
직업도 이름도 벗어놓고
본적도 주소도 벗어놓고
구름처럼 하이얗게 벚꽃 그늘에 앉아보렴
그러면 늘 무겁고 불편한 오늘과
저당 잡힌 내일이
새의 날개처럼 가벼워지는 것을
알게 될 것이다

벚꽃 그늘 아래 한 며칠
두근거리는 생애를 벗어놓아 보렴
그리움도 서러움도 벗어놓고
사랑도 미움도 벗어놓고
바람처럼 잘 씻긴 알몸으로 앉아보렴
더 걸어야 닿는 집도
더 부서져야 완성되는 하루도
동전처럼 초조한 생각도
늘 가볍기만 한 적금통장도 벗어놓고
벚꽃 그늘처럼 청정하게 앉아보렴

Sit down in the Shade of Cherry Blossoms, Please

Please put your life down in the shade of cherry blossoms awhile.
Taking off your clothes and shoes
and throwing off the duty of a father or a husband,
please sit down in nakedness like the brilliant sunbeam.
Forgetting your job or name,
your birthplace or address,
please sit down in the shade of white cherry blossoms
    like the clouds.
Then you will realize
that perpetually heavy, inconvenient today
and mortgaged tomorrow will be as light as
the feathers of a bird.

Please put down your throbbing life for a few days
in the shade of cherry blossoms.
Forgetting either longing or sadness,
love or hatred,
please sit down in nakedness like the clean washed wind.
Along with a house to be reached by further walking on,
a day to be consummated by further collapsing
and a fretful thought like a coin,
throwing off an installment savings passbook that is always

그러면 용서할 것도 용서받은 것도 없는
우리 삶
벌떼 잉잉거리는 벚꽃처럼
넉넉하고 싱싱해짐을 알 것이다
그대, 흐린 삶이 노래처럼 즐거워지길 원하거든
이미 벚꽃 스친 바람이 노래가 된
벚꽃 그늘로 오렴

felt to be light,
please sit down neatly like the shadow of cherry blossoms.

Then, there is nothing forgiving or to be forgiven about
our life.
Like cherry blossoms with a swarm of humming bees,
you will know that life becomes ample and fresh.
If you want a dull life to be enjoyable like a song,
please come in the shade of cherry blossoms
where the wind brushing cherry blossoms has already become
a song.

봄길과 동행하다

움 돋는 풀잎 외에도
오늘 저 들판에는 무슨 일이 일어나고 있는지
꽃 피는 일 외에도
오늘 저 산에는 무슨 일이 일어나고 있는지
종일 풀잎들은 초록의 생각에 빠져있다
들길이 아침마다 파란 수저를 들 때
그때는 우리도 한 번쯤
그리움을 그리워해 볼 일이다
마을 밖으로 달려 나온 어린 길 위에
네 이름도 한 번 쓸 일이다
길을 데리고 그리움을 마중하다 보면
세상이 한 번은 저물고 한 번은 밝아오는
이유를 안다
이런 나절엔 바람의 발길에 끝없이
짓밟혀라도 보았으면
꽃들이 함께 피어나는 것은
세상에서 가장 아름다운 말로
편지를 보내는 것이다
그 꽃의 언어로 편지를 쓰고
나도 너를 찾아
봄길과 동행하고 싶다

Accompanied by a Path in Springtime

Besides the budding of the leaves of grass,
what is happening to the field today?
Besides the blooming of flowers,
what is happening to the mountains today?
All day long, the leaves of grass indulge in thought of
greenness.
When a field path picks up a green spoon and chopsticks
every morning,
then, it is a thing for us to long for longing at least once.
On a little path run out of the village,
it's a thing for you to write your name for once.
While meeting longing in company with the path,
we know why the world gets dark at one time
and dawns at another.
In such a half a day, I wish to be trodden endlessly
by the foot of the winds.
The fact that the flowers are blossoming together
is to send letters
in the most beautiful words in the world.
Writing a letter in the words of a flower
and looking for you,
I wish to accompany a path in springtime.

봄 속에서 길 잃고
봄 속에서 깨어나고 싶다

Getting lost in springtime,
I feel like waking up in springtime.

『가장 따뜻한 책』(2005)에서

From *The Warmest Book*

별이 뜰 때

나는 별이 뜨는 풍경을 삼천 번은 넘게 바라보았다
그런데도 별이 무슨 말을 국수처럼 입에 물고 이 세상 뒤란으로 살금살금 걸어오는지를 말한 적이 없다
별이 뜨기 전에 저녁쌀을 안쳐놓고 상추 뜯으러 나간 누이에 대해 나는 쓴 일이 없다
상추 뜯어 소쿠리에 담아 돌아오는 누이의 발목에 벌레울음이 거미줄처럼 감기는 것을 말한 적이 없다
딸랑딸랑 방울을 흔들며 따라오던 강아지가 옆집 강아지를 만나 어디론가 놀러 가버린 그 고요함을 말한 일이 없다
바삐 갈아 넘긴 머슴의 쟁기에 찢겨 아직도 아파하는 산그늘에 대해,
어서 가야 하는데, 노오란 새끼들이 기다리고 있는데
아직 벌레를 잡지 못해 가슴을 할딱이는 딱새가 제 부리로 가슴 털을 파고 있는 이른 저녁을 말한 일이 없다
곧 서성이던 풀밭들은 침묵할 것이고 나뭇잎들은 다소곳해질 것이다
부엌에는 접시들이 달그락거리며 입 닫은 딱새의 말을 대신해 줄 것이다
별이 뜨면 사방이 어두워져 그 때 막내 별이 숟가락을 입에 문 채 문간으로 나올 거라는 내 생각은 틀림없을 것이다
별이 뜨면 너무 오래 써 너덜너덜해진 천 원짜리 지폐같은 반달이 느리게 느리게 남쪽 산 위로 돋을 것이라는 내 생각은
틀림없을 것이다
별이 뜨면 벌들과 딱정벌레들이 둥치에서 안 떨어지려고 있는 힘을

When Stars Twinkle

I've watched stars twinkling more than three thousands times.
But I've never said that what words like the noodle the stars hold
in their mouths and stealthily walk to the backyard of this world.
I've never written of my sister who had rice get cooked for supper
and went out to pick lettuce before the stars twinkle.
I've never said of insects' chirping coiling like the spiderwebs
round her ankle when she returned with lettuce in a basket.
I've never said of silence at the moment when a puppy tinkling along
after me is gone away to frolic after seeing a neighbour's puppy.
Of the mountain shades torn and still in pain by the plough of a
hasty farmhand; I must go quickly because the yellowish babies
    are waiting.
I've never said of an early evening in which a hungry redstart
panting for breath pecks at feathers on its chest because it did
    not catch an insect yet.
Soon, the fluttering grass field will fall into silence and the leaves
of a tree will be obedient. Rattling dishes in the kitchen will
    speak out on behalf of a silent redstart.
When stars twinkle, it'll be dark all around. Then, my idea that
the last-born star holding a spoon in its mouth will come to the gate
    must be correct.
When stars twinkle, my idea that the half moon, like an old,

다해 나무를 거머쥐고 있는 것을 어둠 속에서 볼 수 있을 것이다
별이 뜨면 귀뚜라미가 찢긴 쌀포대에서 쌀 쏟아지는 소리로 운다고
터무니 없는 말을 나는 한 마디만 더 붙이려고 한다
이것들이 다 별이 뜰 때, 별이 뜨면 생기는 일들이다

worn-out, tattered one thousand won paper money, will rise up slowly and slowly over the mountains in the south,
must be correct.

When stars twinkle, it's possible to watch in the dark that bees and beetles clinging to the trunk not to fall down are clutching
the tree with all their strength.

When stars twinkle, I'll add with the ludicrous words that a cricket chirps as if rice were pouring down from its torn rice
sack.

These are all happenings when stars begin to twinkle or
are twinkling.

따뜻한 책

행간을 지나온 말들이 밥처럼 따뜻하다
한 마디 말이 한 그릇 밥이 될 때
마음의 쌀 씻는 소리가 세상을 씻는다
글자들의 숨 쉬는 소리가 피 속을 지날 때
글자들은 제 뼈를 녹여 마음의 단백이 된다
서서 읽는 사람아
내가 의자가 되어줄게 내 위에 앉아라
우리 눈이 닿을 때까지 참고 기다린 글자들
말들이 마음의 건반 위를 뛰어다니는 것은
세계의 잠을 깨우는 언어의 발자국 소리다
엽록처럼 살아 있는 예지들이
책 밖으로 뛰어나와 불빛이 된다
글자들은 늘 신생을 꿈꾼다
마음의 쟁반에 담기는 한 알 비타민의 말들
책이라는 말이 세상을 가꾼다

The Warm Book

Words passed between lines are warm like boiled rice.
When a word turns to a bowl of boiled rice,
the sound washing the rice of mind cleans up the world.
When the breathing of letters passes through blood,
letters melt their bones into the protein of mind.
A man reading in standing,
please sit down on me as I will be a chair for you.
Letters that have waited for the arrival of our eyes—
words running about on the mind's keyboard are the sounds
of the footstep of a language awaking the sleep of the world.
Like chlorophyl, living sagacity becomes a glow of fire
when it comes out of the book.
Letters dream of a new life all the time.
Words are like a vitamin tablet on the dish of mind;
the word called a book cultivates the world

『나무, 나의 모국어』(2012)에서

From *The Tree, My Mother Tongue*

가을이라는 물질

가을은 서늘한 물질이라는 생각이 나를 끌고 나무나라로 들어간다
잎들에는 광물냄새가 난다
나뭇잎은 나무의 영혼이 담긴 접시다
접시들이 깨지지 않고 반짝이는 것은
나무의 영혼이 담겨 있기 때문이다
햇빛이 금속처럼 내 몸을 만질 때 가을은 물질이 된다
나는 이 물질을 찍어 편지 쓴다
촉촉이 편지 쓰는 물질의 승화는 손의 계보에 편입된다
내 기다림은 붉거나 푸르다
내 발등 위에 광물질의 나뭇잎이 내려왔다는 기억만으로도
나는 한 해를 견딜 수 있다
그러나 너무 오만한 기억은 내 발자국을 어지럽힌다
낙엽은 가을이라는 물질 위에 쓴
나무의 유서다
나는 가을 시 한 편을 낙엽의 무덤 위에 놓아두고
흙 종이에 발자국을 찍으며 돌아온다

A Material Called Autumn

An idea that autumn is a cool material drags me
    into the country of trees.
The leaves of a tree smell of mineral.
The leaves are plates on which the soul of a tree is put.
The fact that the plates are not broken but glistening
says that the soul of a tree is on it.
When the sunlight touches my body like a metal,
    autumn becomes a material.
I write a letter by dipping a pen into this material.
The sublimation of a moistened material for writing a letter
transfers to the lineage of a hand.
My waiting is either red or blue.
With the memory of a mineral tree leaf fallen
on top of my foot only, I can put up with one year.
But an excessively proud memory disturbs my footprints.
A fallen leaf is a will of the tree written on a material
    called autumn.
Putting an autumn poem on the grave of fallen leaves,
I come back while stamping footprints on the earthen paper.

가을 우체국

외롭지 않으려고 길들은 우체국을 세워놓았다
누군가가 배달해 놓은 가을이 우체국 앞에 머물 때
사람들은 저마다 수신인이 되어
가을을 받는다
우체통에 쌓이는 가을 엽서
머뭃이 아름다운 발목들
은행나무 노란 그늘이 우체국을 물들이고
더운 마음에 굽혀 노랗거나 붉어진 시간들
춥지 않으려고 우체통이 빨간 옷을 입고 있다
우체통마다 나비처럼 떨어지는 엽서들
지상의 가장 더운 어휘들이 살을 맞댄다
가을의 말이 은행잎처럼 쌓이는
가을 엽서에는 주소가 없다

A Post Office in Autumn

Lest being lonely, the roads have set up post offices.
When autumn delivered by someone stops before a post office,
each of the people receives autumn
as an addressee.
Postcards in autumn are stacked up in a postbox;
stopping over makes ankles beautiful.
The yellowish shade of a ginkgo tree dyes the post office:
hours baked by a burning heart turn to either yellow or red.
Lest being cold, the postbox puts on red clothes.
Like a butterfly, a postcards falls into the postbox.
The hottest words on earth bring flesh to flesh.
In an autumn postcard that autumnal words file up
    like the leaves of ginkgo,
there is no address.

『꽃들의 화장 시간』(2014)에서

From *At the Makeup Hour of Flowers*

생은 과일처럼 익는다

어떤 열매를 달까 생각느라 나무는 고개를 숙인다
그 힘으로 저녁이면 과일이 익는다
향기는 둥치 안에 숨었다가 조금씩 우리의 코에 스민다
사람 아니면 누구에게 그립다는 말을 전할까
저녁이 숨이 될 때 어둠 속에서 부르는 이름이
생의 이파리가 된다
이름으로 남은 사람들이 내 생의 핏줄이다
하루를 태우고 남은 빛이 별이 될 때
어둡지 않으려고 마을과 집들은 함께 모인다
어느 별에 살다가 내게 온 생이여
내 생은 나 혼자만의 것이 아니구나
나무가 팔을 벋어 다른 나무를 껴 안 듯
사람은 팔을 벋어 타인을 껴안는다
어느 가슴이 그립다는 말을 발명했을까
공중에도 푸른 하루가 살듯이
내 시에는 사람의 이름이 살고 있다
붉은 옷 한 벌 해지면 떠나갈 꽃들처럼
그렇게는 내게 온 생을 떠나보낼 수 없다
귀빈이여 내게 온 생이여
네가 있어 삶은 과일처럼 익는다

Life Ripens Like the Fruit

Musing on what fruit it will bear, the tree bows its head.
By dint of its strength, the fruit ripens in the evening.
Scents lurked in the trunk seep slowly through our nose.
If not a man, to whom shall I send the word "longing"?
When evening turns to a breath, the name called
in darkness becomes a leaf of life.
Those surviving as names are the blood veins of my life.
When light left in the wake of igniting a day into a fire
  turns into stars,
villages and houses gather together to beat darkness.
Life having lived in a star came to me;
my own life is not mine!
Like a tree clasping other trees by stretching its branches,
a man hugs another by extending his mind.
Whose heart has invented the word "longing"?
As a blue day dwells in the air,
a man's name has life in my poem.
Like flowers—when a suit of red clothes wears out—to be gone,
I cannot let my life depart from me.
My honoured guest, life which came to me.
While you are staying, life ripens like the fruit.

그늘은 나무의 생각이다

나무의 생각이 그늘을 만든다
그늘을 넓히고 좁히는 것은 나무의 생각이다
사람들이 아무리 잡아당겨도 나무는
나무가 뻗고 싶은 곳으로 가서 그늘을 만든다
그늘은 일하다가 쉬는 나무의 쉼 자리다
길을 아는가 물으면 대답하지 않고
가고 싶은 곳으로만 가서 제 지닌 만큼의 자유를 심으면서
나무는 가지와 잎의 생각을 따라 그늘을 만든다
수피 속으로 난 길은 숨은 길이어서 나무는
나무 혼자만 걸어 다니는 길을 안다
가지가 펴놓은 수평 아래 아이들이 와서 놀면
나무는 잎을 내려 보내 아이들과 함께 논다
가로와 세로로 짜 늘인 넓은 그늘
그늘은 나무의 생각이다

A Bower Is the Idea of a Tree

The idea of a tree makes a bower.
It's the idea of a tree to broaden or to narrow a bower.
No matter how hard a man jerks at,
the tree makes a bower at the spot where it likes to go.
A bower is a resting place where a tree stops working.
Without answering to the question, "You know where to go?",
the tree goes up where it wishes to go and plants
    as much freedom as it bears;
it makes a bower based on what branches and leaves think.
As the track opened in the bark is a lurked one,
the tree knows how it can walk all alone.
If children come to play under the crown of a tree,
it lowers its leaves and plays with children.
A broad bower woven in a lattice and stretched out;
that is the idea of a tree.

『흰 꽃 만지는 시간』(2017)에서

From *A Time for Fondling the White Flower*

시간

색깔도 무게도 없는 것이 손도 발도 없는 것이 오늘을 만들고 내일을 만들고 영원을 만든다 풀잎을 밀어올리고 강물을 흐르게 하고 단풍을 갈아입는다 누가 그 요람에 앉아 시를 쓰고 노래를 짓고 그림을 그린다 보이지도 만질 수도 없는 저 힘으로

Time

has no colour nor weight nor hands nor feet but makes today or tomorrow or eternity. It pushes up the leaves of grass, lets the river flow and changes into autumnal colours. Someone in its cradle is writing a poem, composing a song and painting a picture with
the power which is neither visible nor touchable.

시인이 걷는 길이
가장 아름다운 길이 되었으면 좋겠다

풀밭은 목차가 없어서 어디서 읽어도 목차다
나뭇잎 한 장에 쓰인 먼 소식을 이틀 동안 아껴 읽는다
오늘이 하루로만 끝나서는 안 된다고 긴 끈을 던져 오후를 문고리에
묶는다

풀잎에게 어서 이불을 덮으라고
어둠 아니면 누가 저리 자상히 일러 줄까

이파리들이 밤에도 잎맥을 만든다는 걸 생각하면
풀잎이라는 말이 성서의 구절보다 경건해진다
그런 땐 꽃을 지우고 난 나무는 무얼 기다릴까가 궁금하다

내 서정은 흰 종이처럼 여려
벌레를 덮어주지도 못하는 헝겊에 말의 수놓으며
오늘도 발에 밟힌 이름들을 생각하다 잠든다

시인이 걸어간 이 길이
가장 아름다운 길이 되었으면 좋겠다

I Wish the Poet's Path to Be a Fairest One

The grassland has no table of contents, so wherever
    you start from, it makes no difference.
I read the news written on one leaf of tree from afar
    while valuing every moment for two days.
Today should not end up only in one day; it ties an afternoon
    to a door-ring by throwing a long string.

If not darkness, who will speak sweetly to the leaves of grass
to cover them quickly with the quilt?

Considered that even the vein of a leaf is made at night,
the word leaf gets more reverential than a biblical passage.
Then, I wonder what a tree is waiting after flowers are gone.

Since my sentiment is as tender as a sheet of white paper,
I stud words on a patch that cannot even tuck an insect.
Musing on the names trampled underfoot, I fall asleep today.

I wish this path that a poet has taken should be
a fairest one.

모르는 사람의 손이 더 따뜻하리라

내일 이 땅에 종말이 온다 해도
나는 화성엔 가지 않을 거야
거기엔 내 좋아하는 참깨와 녹두콩을 심지 못하므로
오늘 핀 도라지꽃 그릴 한 다스의 색연필이 없으므로
일기책 태운 온기에 손 쬐며 쓴 시를
최초의 목소리로 읽어줄 사람 없으므로
지구 아니면 어느 책상에 앉아 아름다운 글을 쓰겠니?
노래가 깨끗이 청소해 놓은 길
어느 방향으로 책상을 놓아
내일 아침의 왼쪽 가슴에 달아줄 이름표를 만들겠니?
생각하는 마음 때문에 세상 한 쪽이 더워진다고 쓴 말을
어디에 보관해야 정오까지 빛나겠니?
샘물이 솟는 곳에서 살고 싶다던 사람을 서서 기다리면
나무에 남은 온기가 절반은 식어도
모르는 사람의 손이 따뜻하리라

Hands of a Stranger Will Be Warmer

Though the end of the world comes to this earth tomorrow,
I won't go to Mars
because I can't sow my favorite sesame and mung beans there,
because there aren't a dozen coloured pencils to draw
　　a bellflower which has bloomed today
and because there is no one who will first read a poem written
by a hand warmed over a fire of burnt diary.
If not on earth, at what desk can I seat and write
　　a beautiful poem?
On the path that a song has cleaned up neatly,
where shall I direct a desk to make a name tag be pinned
on the left chest of tomorrow's morning?
Where am I to keep the written words—one side of the world
will be warmer due to a thinking mind—to shine until noon?
When I wait in standing for one who wished to live
　　where spring water spurts out
and if warmth left on a tree may go cold in half,
the hands of a stranger will get warm.

스무 번째의 별 이름

아름다운 사람을 만나고 온 날은
때 묻은 옷이 깨끗해진다
멀리서 부쳐 온 봉투 안의 소식이
나팔꽃 꽃씨처럼 우편함에 떨어진다
그 소리에 계절이 활짝 넓어진다
인간이 아닌 곳에도 위대한 것이 많이 있다
사소한 삶들이 위대하지 않다고 말할 권리가 나에겐 없다
누구나 제 삶을 묶으면 몇 다발 채소로 요약된다
초록 아니면 보라로 색칠되는 생이 거기 있다
풀꽃의 한 벌 옷에 비기면 내 다섯 벌의 옷은 너무 많다
한 광주리 과일에 한 해를 담아놓고
아름다운 사람은 햇빛을 당겨와 마음을 다림질한다
추운 발자국을 나뭇잎으로 덮어주지 못한 걸 후회하는 사람
파란 이파리 하나를 못 버려 옷깃에 꽂아보는 사람
아름다운 사람은 오늘 밤 스무 번째의 별이름을 짓는다

Name of the Twentieth Star

On the day when I come back from meeting with
    a man of beauty,
the soiled clothes get cleaned up.
News in an envelop sent from a far distance
falls into a mailbox like a seed of morning glory.
To its sound, a season opens widely.
Many of great things exist beyond the human world.
I have no rights to say that a petty life is not great.
If one bundles one's own life, it is surmised
    as a few bundles of vegetables.
There is life coloured in purple if not in green.
Compared with a suit of clothes for a flowering plant,
    five suits of my clothes are too many.
Putting a year in a basketful of the fruit,
a man of beauty draws sunlight and irons out the mind.
A man who regrets for not covering footprints with fallen leaves.
A man who pins it on a collar, for he can't dump a green leaf.
A man of beauty names the twentieth star tonight.

흰 종이 위에

나는 쓴다 흰 종이 위에
내가 지나온 마을 이름을
마을이 내어놓은 가르마길을
흰 종이 위에 나는 쓴다
내가 읽은 책을
김소월 로세티 릴케 쉼보르스카를
연필심이 다 닳도록 나는 쓴다
내가 좋아하는 파란색 덧저고리를
저고리 깃에 반짝이는 하얀 동정을
망개나무 만나러 오르막길 가는
신발소리 유난한 자드락길과
낮에 나온 반달의 흰 눈썹을
연필심을 깎아 다시 쓴다
오래 전 앓다 나은 따스한 병을
내 전부를 다 던지지 못한 젊은 날의 사랑을
물방울꽃을 데리고 왔다 저 혼자 가버리는
내 땅의 봄날을
'사'만 쓰고 '랑'을 못 쓴 미완의 시를!

On the White Paper

On the white paper, I write
the name of a village that I have passed by
and a forked path that the village thrust out.
On the white paper, I write
of the books that I have read.
Kim So-wol°, Rossetti°°, Rilke°°°, Szymborska°°°°
I write of them until a pencil lead runs short;
my favorite blue overwear,
a white cloth-covered collar glittering at neckban,
a steep hilly trail with the unusual noise of rubber shoes
on an ascending road to meet supplejack
and the white brows of the half-moon in daytime.
After sharpening a pencil lead, I write again
of a warm disease cured after a long sickness,
youth's love into which I've never thrown all of myself,
a spring day in my land that brings
a few-flower conehead and goes alone,
and an unfinished poem; only "sa" is written but not "rang"
out of "sarang", love!

° Kim So-wol (1902~1934) was born in Guseong, Pyeonganbuk-do in North Korea. He was best known for his collection of poems *Azaleas* published in 1925.

°° Rossetti was born in 1828 and died in 1882. He was known as Date Gabriel Rossetti. He was a British poet, illustrator and translator.

°°° His full name is René Karl Wilhelm Johann Josef Maria Rilke (1875–1926). He is better known as Rainer Maria Rilke who was a Bohemian-Austrian poet and novelist. He is widely recognized as one of the most lyrically intense German-language poets.

°°°° Szymborska, Wislawa (1923~2012) is a Polish poetess, essayist, translator and recipient of the 1996 Nobel Prize in Literature.

목백일홍 옛집

연필을 놔두고 나온 것 같다
빨랫줄에 걸린 수건에는 지나가던 소식들이 자주 걸렸다
늘 정직하기만 한 과꽃과의 이별
내가 떠나는데도 눈빛이 맑던 쟁반
피부가 하얀 접시
깨어지면서도 음악이 되던 보시기
마음을 접고 펴던 살 부러진 우산
화요일과 목요일의 날개에 아무 차이가 없는 나비
자고 나면 새 아이들을 데리고 나오는 나무
나쁜 이파리라고는 하나도 없는 집을
나는 신던 신발을 신고 너무 멀리 걸어나왔다
나 없어 혼자 놀다가는 사금파리에 담긴 정오
목백일홍은 전화를 못 받아서
안부를 물을 수도 없는 지금

An Old House with Crape-myrtle

Methinks, I left a pencil behind.
A passing news is often netted by the towel on a washing line.
Parting from an aster that is always honest.
Though I'm leaving, the glittering eyes of a tray are clear.
A dish whose skin is white.
At the time of being broken, a small brass bowl is used
    to be music.
An umbrella folding or unfolding mind with its broken ribs.
A butterfly with no difference from Tuesday's wings to
    Thursday's.
The tree bringing out new siblings after one night sleep.
Being shodden, I walked out too far away from the house
with no bad leaf at all.
The midday going away after playing alone in my absence
    is held in porcelain chips.
As crape-myrtle is unable to receive telephone,
it is now that it cannot ask after one's health.

나무를 눕히는 방법

나무는 일생 서 있어서 나무다
나무도 한 번은 눕고 싶을 것이다
누가 서 있는 나무의 편안을 도모하리
누가 저 나무에게 휴식을 가르치리
기를 쓰고 이를 악물고 사는 날까지
제가 서 있다는 것도 모르고 서있다
누가 도끼로 때려눕히기 전에는 절대로
나무이기를 포기하지 않고 나무는 서 있다
누가 저 나무에게 안식을 권하리
햇빛의 식사를 포기하기 전에는
톱으로 잘라 둥치를 땅에 눕히기 전에는

A Way of Laying a Tree Down

The tree is the tree because it stands in its all life.
The tree may wish to lie down once in life.
Who can promote the comfort of the standing tree?
Who can teach recess to the tree?
Exerting every effort and clenching its teeth until the end of life,
the tree does stand without knowing of its standing.
Before someone chops the tree down with an axe,
it is standing without forsaking its identity as a tree.
Who could possibly commend solace to the tree?
— before giving up the meals of sunlight
and laying the trunk down by sawing.

채송화 수첩

봄 볕살 하나마다 이불 한 채씩 내걸면 잘 마르겠다
나비들은 제 한 벌뿐인 옷을 자랑하고 싶어서
그늘을 벗어놓고 햇빛으로 날아 나온다
벌들은 드난살이가 오래여서 눈이 붉어졌다
꽃이 조명등처럼 떨어진다
아무리 예쁜 꽃나무라도 시를 열지는 않는다는 걸
알고 난 뒤부터 채송화를 햇빛 색종이라 부르지 않게 되었다
이 작은 수첩에 봄날의 마음을 다 쓸 수는 없다
비워 둔 말은 배고픈 새가 와 쪼아 먹도록 남겨 둔다

A Jotter for Rose Moss

If a cotton duvet is put in each beam of spring sunlight,
    it is likely to be well dried.
Craving for showing off their glad rags,
butterflies fly into sunlight after taking off the shade.
Bee's eyes turned red after a long life of an itinerant.
Flowers fall down like street lamps.
Knowing that even the loveliest floral tree does not bear a poem,
I have come not to call rose moss as the colored paper of sunlight.
In this small jotter, I cannot jot down the whole mind
    of a spring day.
I have saved the vacant words for a hungry bird to peck at.

미수록 시편에서

From *Uncollected Poems*

근심을 지펴 밥을 짓는다

꽃씨 떨어지는 세상으로 내려가
꽃씨보다 더 작게 살고 싶었다
나뭇잎이 지면서 남긴 이야기를 모아 동화를 쓰고
병에서 깨어나는 사람의 엷은 미소를 보며
시를 쓰고 싶었다
저 혼자 나들이 간 마음이 날개가 찢겨 돌아올 때마다
가제 손수건으로 피 묻은 그의 얼굴을 닦아주었다
어린 근심아
강을 못 건너고 돌아오는 네 얼굴의 슬픔
더 멀리 가려던 네 꿈이 새의 죽지처럼 꺾였구나
들판이 강물을 보듬고
남은 햇살이 하루를 껴안을 때
너의 몸이 종이쪽처럼 가벼워졌구나
악의를 씻어 국 끓이고 가시로 돋는 증오를 빗질하면
어느덧 마음 한 켠에 파랗게 돋는 새 잎
모래의 마음이 숲이 되는 날을 기다려
내 손수 지은 색동옷 갈아입히면
칭얼대던 근심들이 하얀 쌀밥이 되어 밥상에 오른다
그때 나는 너에게 상처를 보석이라고
슬픔은 실밥 따뜻한 내복이라고
이 세상 가장 긴 편지를 쓰리라
근심이 눈발처럼 흩날려도

Cooking Rice by Burning Anxiety as Firewood

Coming down to the world where a flower seed falls,
I wished to live pettier life than that of the seed.
Writing a fairy tale by collecting stories left by falling leaves
and looking at a faint smile of the sick rallying from illness,
I wished to write a poem.
Whenever the mind returned—after going out alone—
    with its broken wings,
I cleaned up its blood-stained face with a gauze handkerchief.
A benign anxiety,
grief on your face when you return without crossing the river,
your dream of further going away is broken
    like the joint of a bird's wing!
When the field hugs the river
and the rest of sunlight cuddles the day,
your body has turned light like a sheet of paper!
Boiling soup by washing malice and combing thorny hatred,
a new green leaf, unawares, buds at the corner of the mind.
If I wait for the day when the mind of sand turns to gold
and dress it with rainbow-striped clothes sewn by my own hands,
a whining anxiety becomes white cooked rice and is served
    on the dining table.
Then, calling the wound as a gem

날개 찢긴 근심이 돌아와 갈아입을 옷 한 벌
다림질하리라
슬픔이 아닌, 눈물이 아닌
환하고 따뜻한 이야기를 모닥불처럼 나누리라

and grief as underclothes made of warm thrum,
I will write the longest letter in the world.
Though anxiety flutters like the flake of snow,
I will iron out a suit of clothes for a change
when anxiety with its broken wings comes back.—
I will share a bright, warm tale—neither grief
    nor tears—like a bonfire.

아침 언어

저렇게 빨간 말을 토하려고
꽃들은 얼마나 지난밤을 참고 지냈을까
뿌리들은 또 얼마나 이파리를 재촉했을까
그 빛깔에 닿기만 해도 얼굴이 빨갛게 물드는
저 뜨거운 꽃들의 언어

하루는 언제나 어린 아침을 데리고 온다
그 곁에서 풀잎이 깨어나고
밤은 별의 잠옷을 벗는다

아침만큼 자신만만한 얼굴은 없다
모든 신생이 거기 있기 때문이다
초록이 몸속으로 스며드는 아침 곁에서
사람을 기다려 보면 즐거우리라

내 기다리는 모든 사람에게 꽃의 언어를 주고 싶지만
그러나 꽃의 언어는 번역되지 않는다

나무에서 길어낸 그 말은
나무처럼 신선할 것이다
초록에서 길어낸 그 말은
이 세상 가장 아름다운 모음일 것이다

Words at Morn

To spew out such red words,
how much did the flowers hold back last night?
How much did the roots push the leaves up, too?
On being touched by the colour, faces turn red—
those burning words of flowers.

A day always brings with the infant morn.
Beside it, the leaves of grass wake up
and night undresses a starry nightgown.

No face is so proud as the morn
because all new life dwells in it.
Beside the morn when green soaks into the body,
waiting for a man will be a thing of joy.

Though I wish to give words of flowers to all men in waiting,
the words of flowers do not yield to translation.

The words grown out of the tree will be fresh
like the tree.
The word grown out of green will be
the most beautiful vowel in the world.

새똥

새는 예쁜 꽃에는 똥을 누지 않는다
저도 사랑하는 입술이 있기 때문이다

Bird's Droppings

A bird does not mute on the petals of a lovely flower;
for it has also its loving lips.

Kee-Chul Lee (1943~)
Poet and literary scholar

Life and Works of Kee-Chul Lee

1943. Kee-Chul Lee was born on the 9th of January at Seokgang-ri, Gajo-myeon, Geochang-gun, Gyeongsangnam-do, Republic of Korea. He was the second son among five children of Lee Myeong-ui and Park Sun-ju.

1955. When he was a juvenile, he had a keen interest in the subject of Korean Language in the school curriculum. On the day he received the Korean language textbook in his middle school years, he read through the textbook in a single day and memorized every poem in the textbook. Especially, he loved to recite the poems such as Kim Kwang-seop's "Mind", Park Du-jin's "The Tree" and "The Sun", the entire poems in *Azaleas* by Kim So-wol, and "Chanson d'automne" by Paul Verlaine (This part of life is recorded in the first and second chapters of the poet's autobiographical novel titled *Days on Earth*).

1958. Enters Joongang Highschool in Geochang, Gyeongsangnam-do, South Korea

1960. The April 19 Student Uprising was in his senior year at highschool. Wins the first prize with the poem entitled "A Bird" in the poetry writing competition held in May at the Arim Arts Festival (Arim is the ancient name of Geochang).

1962. Admitted to the Department of Korean Language and Literature, College of Liberal Arts, Yeungnam University, in Daegu, Gyeongsangbuk-do, South Korea. Studies Korean literature under the tutelage of Lee Jae-Cheol, the theorist of children's literature.

1963. In his sophomore, receives a literary award at the nation-wide collegiate poetry contest hosted by Kyungpook National University in Daegu. Meets the renowned poet Chun-su Kim in his office for the first time who made some influence on his poems. Around 1964, starts to contribute critical essays to the *simunhak* (*The Poetic Literature*).

1967. Short listed for the annual spring literary contest with the poem titled "Trakl's Ward" in the poetry division hosted by the *Jung-ang Ilbo*. Joins the army and discharged from military duty in 1970.

1971. Graduates from Yeungnam University with a BA in Korean Language and Literature.

1972. Completes the requirements of becoming a poet with the recommendations of three poems, "deulleun gohyang" ("Stopping by Hometown"), "neowa hamkkae" ("With You"), and "Gohyangsi" ("Poems on Hometown") through the *Hyundae Munhak* (*Modern Literature*).

1974. First collection of poems titled *nanmal chujeok* (*Word Chase*) published at the poet's own expense. Receives an MA degree with a thesis titled "A Methodological Study of Modern Korean Poetry" from the Graduate School of Yeungnam University.

1976. Becomes a member of a poetry coterie, *Jayusi* (Free Verse).

1978. In the summer issue of the *Segyemunhak* (*The World Literature*), five poems were published. These poems attract some attention from poets and critics such as Dong-gyu Hwang and Ha-rim Choi. Their reviews were published in the *Chosun Ilbo* and the *Hyundae Munhak*, respectively. Admitted to the Graduate School of Yeungnam University as a doctoral candidate in Korean Language and Literature. Takes a position at Pohang College as a full-time lecturer.

1979. From this year on, the eco-friendly poems such as "seojjogeuro gamyeon" ("If You Go Westward"), "chorogeul bomyeo" ("Looking at Green"), and "jjokduri kkochi jineun nal" ("The Day When Cyclamen Falls off") were continuously published in the *Segyemunhak* (*The World Literature*).

1980. Transferred to the Department of Korean Language and Literature at Masan University as a full-time lecturer.

1981. Transferred to the Dept of Korean Language and Literature at Yeungnam University from Masan University to fill a vacancy held by the late professor poet Chun-su Kim.

1982. Through Korea University Professor U-chang Kim's good offices, *Cheongsanhaeng* (*Lines Composed for the Blue Mountains*), the second volume of collected poems, was published by Mineumsa, and the *Collected Poems of Lee Sang-hwa* was published by Munjangsa.

1985. Through Ju-yeon Kim's good offices, *jeonjaengkwa pyonghwa* (*War and Peace*), the 3rd volume of collected poems, was published by Munhakkwajiseongsa. Visits to Tokyo,

Tsukuba, Kyoto, Nara and Nagoya in Japan.

1986. Receives a doctorate degree with the dissertation titled *A Study of Lee Sang-hwa* from the Graduate School of Yeungnam University. Receives the Daegu Munhaksang (Daegu Literary Award).

1988. *Usuui ibureul deopgo* (*Covering with the Quilt of Melancholy*), the 4th volume of collected poems, was published by Mineumsa. Visits to Russia, Hungary, the Czecho Republic, and Germany. Publishes *Munhwa Bipyeong* (*Cultural Criticism*), a general magazine for culture, in Daegu for five years as the editor and publisher.

1989. Through Kim Si-tae's good offices, *nae sarangeun haejineun yeongtoe* (*My Love Is in the Realm Where the Sun Sets*), the 5th volume of collected poems, was published by Munhakkwabipyeongsa.

1990. A book of poetic theory, *A Quest for Poetry*, was published by Simsangsa.

1991. The sixth volume of collected poems titled *simin ilgi* (*Citizen's Diary*) was published by Urimunhaksa.

1992. *A History of Modern Korean Personage: Lee Sang-hwa* was published by the publishing department of the *Dong-a Ilbo*. Receives the Hukwang Literary Award.

1993. The 7th volume of collected poems, *jisangeseo bureugo sipeun norae* (*Song That I Wish to Sing on Earth*) was published by Munhakkwajiseongsa. Receives a literary award called

Kim Su-yeong Literary Award. Receives Geumbokmun-hwayesulsang and Docheon Literary Award in November. Serves the Daegu Society of Korean Poets for two years as president.

1994. A novel, *ttangwieui naldeul* (*Days on Earth*), was published by Mineumsa. The editorial department of Mineumsa called this novel an "autobiographical novel".

1995. Visits to the State University of New York at Stony Brook with the grant from the Korea Research Foundation as a visiting professor for a year. Makes friends with Korean literary men living in New York and gives lectures on Korean literature to literary men in New York. Travels to the 45 states of the USA with his wife by car. Visits to Canada and Mexico. The 8th volumes of collected poems, *yeolhareul hyanghayeo* (*Towards Jehol*), was published by Mineumsa.

1997. Selected poems titled *cheongsanhaeng* were published by Mineumsa.

1998. The 9th volume of collected poems, *yuriui nanal* (*Days of Glass*), was published by Munhakkwajiseongsa in March. Receives the siwasihaksang (Poetry and Poetics Award) in October. Serves Hanminjokeomunhakhoe, an academic society for studying Korean language and literature, as president. In July, *gahokage geuriun ireum* (*A Severely Longing Name*) and a collection of critical essays *inganjuui bipyeongeul wihayeo* (*For the Criticism of Humanism*) were published by Joeunnal.

1999. A collection of essays, *sonsugeone ssan pyeonji* (*Letters Wrapped by a Handkerchief*), was published by Moadeurim in August.

2000. The 10th volume of collected poems, *naega mannan sarameun modu areumdwotda* (*Those Whom I have Met Were All Beautiful*), was published by Mineumsa in August.

2001. Wins the first literary award of "Choe Gye-rak Munhak-sang" (Choe Gye-rak Literary Award) in November.

2003. Builds the Yeohyangyeowon at Deokchon-ri, Gakbuk-myeon, Cheongdo-gun, Gyeongsangbuk-do, South Korea, and opens "si gakkuneun maeul" (a village for cultivating poetry). This house was built to provide "an intellectual space for discoursing literature and life" in the local area.

2004. The eleventh volume of collected poems, *seumu sarege* (*To the Twenty-year Old*), was published by Sumilwon in June.

2005. The 12th volume of collected poems, *gajang ttatteuthan chaek* (*The Warmest Book*) was published by Mineumsa in January and a collection of essays, *sseulsseulhan goseneun siini itda* (*There Is a Poet in a Lonely Place*), was published by Munhakdongne in August.

2006. The 13th volume of collected poems, *jeongoui sullye* (*Pilgrimage at Noon*), was published by Aeji in August.

2007. The first volume of children's verse, *namuneun jeulgeowo* (*The Tree Is Merry*), was published by Biryongso in October.

2008. Retires from teaching at Yeungnam University in February and becomes a professor emeritus. Travels to

England and Ireland from the 17th of June to the 22nd of July. The 14th volume of collected poems, *saramgwa hamkke i gireul georeonne* (*I Walked on This Road with Others*), was published by Seojeongsihak in August.

2011. The sixteenth volume of collected poems of *ip, ip, ip* (*Leaf, Leaf, Leaf*) was published by Seojeongsihak in October. Travelogue, *yeonggukmunhakui supeul geonilda—dongseo-yangui bereul jjada* (*Roaming amid the Forest of English Literature—Weaving Hemp Cloth between the East and the West*), was published by Puleunsasangsa in November.

2012. The handwritten volume of collected poems, *byeolkkajineun gayahanda* (*Up to the Stars Must We go*), was published by jisigeul mandeuneun jisik in January. The sixteenth volume of collected poems, *namu, naui mogugeo* (*The Tree, My Mother Tongue*), was published by Mineumsa in February.

2014. Thc 17th volume of collected poems, *kkotdeurui hwajangsigan* (*At the Makeup Hour of Flowers*), was published by Seojeongsihak in April.

2015. The three poems, "ttatteutan chaek" (The Warm Book), "cheongsanhaeng" (Lines Composed for the Blue Mountains), and "ne keollyeui sinbal" (Four Pairs of Shoes) were included in the textbook, *Korean Language II*, for Korean highschool students.

2017. The latest 18th volume of collected poems, *huinkkot manjineun sigan* (*A Time for Fondling the White Flower*), was published by Mineumsa in May.

About the Translator

Dr. Jeo-Yong Noh studied English Literature at Pusan National University for his BA (1973) and at the Graduate School of Sogang University for an MA (1977) in South Korea. He was also educated at the Graduate School of Boston College as well as Old Dominion University for his second Master's degree in English Literature (1984). After his studies in the States, he moved to the UK in 1985 to study English Literature and was awarded DPhil in English Literature from the University of Oxford in 1991. Since 1994, he had taught twentieth century Anglo-American poetry at Yeungnam University in Gyeongsan, South Korea until his retirement in 2013.

Professor Noh has published several scholarly books in English including *Biographical Themes in T. S. Eliot's Early Poetry* (1985), *T. S. Eliot and the* Criterion (1999) and *"Action Française" Condemnation & Other Essays* (2003) among others. He served the T. S. Eliot Society of Korea as president from 2003 to 2005. His acclaimed English translation of Korean poems entitled *Korean Buddhist Poems* was published by the Yeungnam University Press in 2006. He also translated *Omeros* by Derek Walcott (1994) and *Ronald Stuart Thomas: Collected Poems 1945-1990* into Korean for the first time (2012).